AF901310

Unive
R

WITHDRAWN
University of
Reading Library

90 0822310 X

$ICMA

Palgrave Studies in Economic History

Series Editor
Kent Deng
London School of Economics
London, UK

Palgrave Studies in Economic History is designed to illuminate and enrich our understanding of economies and economic phenomena of the past. The series covers a vast range of topics including financial history, labour history, development economics, commercialisation, urbanisation, industrialisation, modernisation, globalisation, and changes in world economic orders.

More information about this series at
http://www.palgrave.com/gp/series/14632

Linda Arch

The Regulation of the London Clearing Banks, 1946–1971

Stability and Compliance

palgrave
macmillan

Linda Arch
University of Reading
Reading, UK

University of Reading Library
University of Reading Library

Palgrave Studies in Economic History
ISBN 978-3-030-00909-0 ISBN 978-3-030-00910-6 (eBook)
https://doi.org/10.1007/978-3-030-00910-6

Library of Congress Control Number: 2018956818

© The Editor(s) (if applicable) and The Author(s), under exclusive licence to Springer Nature Switzerland AG 2018
This work is subject to copyright. All rights are solely and exclusively licensed by the Publisher, whether the whole or part of the material is concerned, specifically the rights of translation, reprinting, reuse of illustrations, recitation, broadcasting, reproduction on microfilms or in any other physical way, and transmission or information storage and retrieval, electronic adaptation, computer software, or by similar or dissimilar methodology now known or hereafter developed.
The use of general descriptive names, registered names, trademarks, service marks, etc. in this publication does not imply, even in the absence of a specific statement, that such names are exempt from the relevant protective laws and regulations and therefore free for general use.
The publisher, the authors and the editors are safe to assume that the advice and information in this book are believed to be true and accurate at the date of publication. Neither the publisher nor the authors or the editors give a warranty, express or implied, with respect to the material contained herein or for any errors or omissions that may have been made. The publisher remains neutral with regard to jurisdictional claims in published maps and institutional affiliations.

Cover illustration: © Melisa Hasan

This Palgrave Pivot imprint is published by the registered company Springer Nature Switzerland AG
The registered company address is: Gewerbestrasse 11, 6330 Cham, Switzerland

To Liz and Henry

Acknowledgements

The author wishes to thank the Bank of England and the Conservative Party for permission to use material from records for which they hold the copyright. The author also wishes to thank the archivists at the Bank of England Archive, the Conservative Party Archive, Lloyds Banking Group Archive, the London Metropolitan Archives, the London School of Economics and Political Science Library, Archives and Special Collections and the National Archives for their assistance.

This book contains public sector information licensed under the Open Government Licence v3.0. The information concerned relates to Crown copyright material created by civil servants, ministers and government departments and agencies.

Contents

Abbreviations

BoE	Bank of England Archive
CCC	Competition and Credit Control
CIC	Capital Issues Committee
CLCB	Committee of London Clearing Bankers
GDP	Gross Domestic Product
IMF	International Monetary Fund
LBGA	Lloyds Banking Group Archive
LMA	London Metropolitan Archives
LSE	London School of Economics and Political Science Library, Archives and Special Collections
NBPI	National Board for Prices and Incomes
OECD	The Organisation for Economic Co-operation and Development
SSDS	Supplementary Special Deposits Scheme
TNA	National Archives
UK	United Kingdom of Great Britain and Northern Ireland
US	United States of America

List of Figures

List of Tables

CHAPTER 1

Introduction

Abstract This chapter sets the scene by observing that the twenty-five to thirty years after the Second World War was a period of unusual stability in banking, in the UK and in many other countries. Focusing upon a group of banks called the "London clearing banks", this book explores the regulation of those banks in the period from 1946 until the early 1970s. It introduces some of the literature on the regulation of clearing banking, pointing out that the dominant interpretation suggests that stability in banking was achieved at the expense of competition. The literature also holds that the approach to regulation was largely driven by a policy of "financial repression". The book questions aspects of this interpretation.

Keywords Clearing banks · London clearing banks · Stability in banking · Financial repression

The period from 1946 until the early 1970s was a period of stability in banking in the UK and one in which there was a high degree of compliance with regulation. During the 1970s, in contrast, the banking system became less stable as the post-war regulatory framework disintegrated or was dismantled, and in December 1973 a crisis of the secondary banks broke. The stable earlier period also stands in contrast to the period since the 1970s, which has been more prone to banking crises, most

© The Author(s) 2018

L. Arch, *The Regulation of the London Clearing Banks, 1946–1971*, Palgrave Studies in Economic History,
https://doi.org/10.1007/978-3-030-00910-6_1

notably the global financial crisis of 2007–2009. The primary purpose of this book is to contribute to our understanding of the nature of clearing bank regulation in the earlier stable period from 1946 until the early 1970s.

The focus of this study is a specific group of banks referred to as the London clearing banks. Who and what were these banks? In 1946, at the beginning of the period under review, there were eleven London clearing banks (Barclays; Coutts & Co.; District; Glyn, Mills & Co.; Lloyds; Martins; Midland; National; National Provincial; Westminster; and Williams Deacon's).[1] In 1962, National Provincial acquired District Bank reducing the number to ten. There was then a flurry of merger activity in the late 1960s, with the mergers of National Provincial with Westminster in 1968, Barclays with Martins, and the merger in 1969 of three smaller clearing banks, Williams Deacon's, Glyn, Mills & Co. and National to form Williams & Glyn's Bank Limited. By 1970, six London clearing banks remained: Barclays, Coutts & Co., Lloyds, Midland, National Westminster and Williams & Glyn's. The term "clearing bank" is rarely used today but the clearing banks were what would now be thought of as retail banks. These banks were termed "clearing banks" because of their membership of the London Bankers' Clearing House. On a daily basis, cheques between the clearing banks were exchanged at the London Bankers' Clearing House, and balances between them were settled. As *London* clearing banks, these banks were required to have a principal office in London, a legacy of London's position as a leading international financial centre during the nineteenth century and up to the First World War.[2] It did not mean that their operations were confined to London. The relative size of the eleven London clearing banks at the beginning of the period based on the value of their current, deposit and other accounts is illustrated in Table 1.1.

Why focus on this particular group of banks? The reason for a focus on the London clearing banks is that for most of this period the London clearing banks were the dominant group of banks within the UK banking sector on a number of measures. They were, for example, the dominant group of banks by assets.[3] They were the primary source of loans and advances: as at mid-December 1964 the London clearing banks were responsible for 67.3% of the £7.4 billion of bank lending to UK residents, excluding lending to other banks.[4]

Given that the stability of the banking system is a key guiding principle of bank regulation, it follows that a very stable period should be of

Table 1.1 London clearing banks' current, deposit and other accounts, 1944

Clearing bank	*Current, deposit and other accounts 1944 (£)*
Midland Bank	1,002,825,685
Barclays Bank	917,775,560
Lloyds Bank	819,285,356
Westminster Bank	598,934,131
National Provincial Bank	589,911,940
Martins Bank	204,264,101
District Bank	169,736,171
Williams Deacon's Bank	80,471,749
Glyn, Mills & Co.	62,576,130
National Bank	56,324,458
Coutts & Co.	38,971,424

Source: *The Bankers' Almanac and Year Book for 1945–1946*, xlvii–xlviii

interest to historians, policymakers and regulators. Reinhart and Rogoff, based on their analysis of sixty-six countries, showed that the absence of banking crises from the 1940s until the early 1970s was a noticeable feature of many banking systems.[5] Grossman has suggested that this period "constitutes the longest sustained period of banking stability this industrialized world has ever known."[6] Alan M. Taylor observed in 2010: "the post-war period of financial repression (including capital controls but also strict regulation of domestic finance) was a remarkable era in combining rapid economic growth and high investment with a crisis-free but strictly regulated and supervised financial system in most countries. This is a remarkable historical fact that warrants further study."[7] The start date of the study—1946—was significant as the year in which the Bank of England Act was enacted by the Labour government under Prime Minister Clement Attlee. Among other things, the Act established the regulatory relationship between banks on the one hand and the Bank of England and the Treasury on the other. The study ends in 1971 with the Bank of England's radical new policy of Competition and Credit Control (CCC). During the 1970s, the UK and other countries experienced a decline in the stability of their banking systems. In 1973–1974, for example, there were several bank failures, particularly but not exclusively in Europe and North America—as detailed in Table 1.2.[8]

This greater fragility in banking systems was not a temporary phenomenon: bank failures and financial crises were to occur more frequently in

Table 1.2 Bank failures, 1973–1974

Date	*Bank(s) involved*
December 1973	United States National Bank of San Diego was declared insolvent and its assets were acquired by The Crocker National Bank of San Francisco
December 1973	The UK secondary banking crisis began
1974	While they did not fail, large foreign exchange losses were experienced at UBS, Westdeutsche-Landesbank Girozentrale, Hessische Landesbank Girozentrale (which had a large stake in the International Credit Bank of Geneva) and Lloyds Bank International
June 1974	On 26 June 1974 the Bankhaus ID Herstatt in the Federal Republic of Germany went bankrupt as a result of losses on foreign exchange transactions
August 1974	A private bank, Bass & Herz of Frankfurt in the Federal Republic of Germany, became insolvent
August 1974	The Israel-British Bank (London) Ltd. suspended payments following the liquidation of its parent, the Israel-British Bank. The subsidiary eventually received support from the Bank of England and the Bank of Israel
September 1974	Banca Privata Italiana was put into liquidation
October 1974	The Franklin National Bank (the twelfth largest bank in the United States) failed on 8 October, in part as a result of foreign exchange trading losses. Franklin was one of four insured banks which failed in the United States in 1974, the others being American Bank & Trust, Orangeburg, South Carolina; Tri-City Bank, Warren, Michigan; and Cromwell State Savings Bank, Cromwell, Iowa[a]
October 1974	On 11 October 1974 the International Credit Bank of Geneva is closed after a run on deposits

[a]"Annual Report of the Federal Deposit Insurance Corporation 1974," Table 3, accessed 24 July 2018, https://www.fdic.gov/about/strategic/report/archives/fdic-ar-1974.pdf

the period from the 1970s until the global financial crisis in 2007–2009 than in the preceding quarter-century. As Bordo and Meissner have noted, "After the breakdown of the Bretton Woods system and the liberalization of global financial markets, as well as domestic financial systems across the world, the stage was set for waves of systemic financial and fiscal crises."[9]

Against this backdrop, how has clearing banking and the regulation of the London clearing banks been interpreted in the literature? The dominant interpretation has tended to hold that clearing banking in the twenty-five to thirty years after the Second World War was undynamic, excessively risk-averse, prone to inertia and slow to innovate. These weaknesses are attributed primarily to a lack of competition in clearing banking. Shielded from competition, the clearing banks had no incentive to innovate. Capie and Billings' succinctly summarize the prevailing interpretation of clearing banking in the literature thus:

> It has long been contended that British commercial banking, for most of the twentieth century, was not competitive; it has sometimes been described as a 'complex' or 'collusive' oligopoly. This is said to account for the banks' allegedly sluggish, conservative and inefficient behaviour - part of the capital market failure that was said to contribute to Britain's relative economic decline.[10]

Moreover:

> It is generally believed that English banks failed to finance industry in as supportive a way as their European contemporaries, discriminated against small firms (and hence implicitly new but more risky enterprises), and suffered from many other defects.[11]

It should be pointed out Capie and Billings do not themselves concur with this interpretation in all respects. In addition to an interpretation of the clearing banking system as rather dysfunctional, historians have argued that the fundamental force shaping the nature of bank regulation was the fact that successive governments needed to minimize the cost of government borrowing, the UK having emerged from the Second World War with a high debt-to-GDP ratio. In 1945, the ratio stood at 225%.[12] Motivated solely or predominantly by self-interest, governments prioritized minimizing the cost of government debt. This necessitated a policy of "financial repression" which operated through the clearing banking system. This tendentious term refers to:

> official policies that direct to government use (and usually at below-market rates) funds that would otherwise go to other borrowers [...] Policies include directed lending to the government by captive domestic audiences (such as pension funds or domestic banks), explicit or implicit caps on interest rates, regulation of cross-border capital movements, and (generally) a tighter connection between government and banks, either explicitly through public ownership of some of the banks or through heavy "moral suasion."[13]

While financial repression may have led to stability in banking, it also led to inertia and excessive risk-aversion it is argued. For their part, the London clearing banks, similarly motivated solely or predominantly by self-interest, accepted financial repression in exchange for restrictions on competition (they were permitted, for example, to set certain prices collectively until 1971). Regulatory policy in this period, according to this interpretation, could be seen to as an expression of the "political bargaining model" of policymaking in which policy is the outcome of "a *game* between *players* occupying positions."[14]

The fact that there was a long period of stability in clearing banking, and that there were high levels of compliance with regulation, is given less attention in the literature than the perceived weaknesses of the banking system, especially the absence of competition. Thus, many historians are highly critical of the motives, intentions and actions of the London clearing banks and the regulator. This view has prevailed even in the wake of the global financial crisis, 2007–2009. The following examples, the majority of which are taken from publications since the crisis, illustrate different aspects of the dominant interpretation. Turner characterizes the regulatory relationship in banking in this period thus: "the government attempted to regulate the financial system to generate low nominal rates and negative real-interest rates, thereby reducing the government's debt-servicing costs and the real value of its debt." The outcome of this contract between the government and the banks was stability because under it banks were prevented from accepting credit risk.[15] In a similar vein, Allen asserts that in order to reduce government debt, a policy of financial repression was adopted. This policy was designed to "prevent people and companies from using their financial assets as they chose."[16] The clearing banks were thus the instruments of financial repression. Reveley and Singleton argue that bank stability was the outcome of the "system of regulated banking designed to facilitate government borrowing and ensure financial stability," and that the Committee of London Clearing Bankers (CLCB) was until 1971 simply "an organizational vehicle for supporting the rent-seeking activities of its clearing bank members."[17] Needham characterizes the regulatory framework before 1971 as "chaotic" and "byzantine."[18]

As for the banking industry itself, Michie describes the years 1945–1970 as being marked by a "high degree of inertia and conservatism," and observes that "it was as if the British banking system had been 'frozen in time' and that time was 1922."[19] Grossman observes that "banking did not change very much in the three decades following the outbreak of World War II."[20] Ackrill and Hannah title the chapter of their history of Barclays Bank about the period 1945–1961, "Stability or Stagnation?"[21] They ascribe the lack of dynamism in the industry to the "somewhat ambiguous, satisficing, collaborative bankers' objectives of the 1960s."[22] Baker and Collins contend that the clearing banks' traditional practice of overdraft lending (as opposed to "term" lending over a set period of time) meant that they accepted very little credit risk. While on the one hand, this led to "a degree of systemic stability that was the envy of the world," it also created a culture in which the clearing banks were incapable of change because they adhered to an "outdated mental model of the market" which itself sprang from "industry-wide cognitive inertia."[23] This "cognitive inertia" led to a "failure to recognize competitive threats and opportunities."[24] Banking, posits Thompson, had changed very little since the Edwardian era, at which point the clearing banks began to consolidate, and to ossify into "giant slow-moving pyramidal corporations."[25] Ross asserts that in the 1950s, "the cocoon in which the government wrapped the British banking structure not only stifled innovation and development of new services and products, but left it completely unable to respond to the competitive pressures of the following decade."[26] Davies suggests that the underlying banking business model itself, based on the asset management theory of banking, was inherently unprofitable and undynamic, in comparison with the business model which succeeded it based on the theory of liability management.[27] Bátiz-Lazo and Wardley on the other hand contest aspects of the dominant interpretation, rejecting the idea that "the major British clearing banks were managed ineffectively by conservative and technically naïve executive officers."[28]

A recurrent theme within the literature is whether the London clearing banks may have failed industry—and thus contributed to the UK's relative economic decline after the war—by not providing funding to business, particularly small and medium enterprises. Collins and Baker's analysis of a sample of 2138 successful applications to banks for funding in the period 1950–1968 reveals that only 5.1% of funding granted was in the form of loans while 53.7% took the form of overdrafts—a more insecure form of borrowing (from the borrower's perspective).[29] Their study, they assert, confirms the "transaction banking nature of English commercial bank provision of finance to the business sector."[30]

Carnevali suggests that because of the highly concentrated and centralized structure of clearing banking in the UK, stability was achieved at the expense of providing finance to small firms.[31] Her argument compares and contrasts the system in the UK with the more heterogeneous and/or decentralized systems in Germany, France and Italy. This view is however contested by Ross who points out that much overdraft lending was akin to medium- or long-term loans because more often than not it was renewed as required.[32] Indeed, the clearing banks "were important and reliable as providers of funds to their customers [...] bank funding of industry was a vital component of the recipient company's overall financial situation."[33] The criticism that the banks failed to support industry can be seen as one strand of a much broader critique of the relationship between the City and industry. In 1984, Ingham coined the term the "City-Bank of England-Treasury nexus" to describe a nexus which privileged the interests of finance over industry.[34]

Several aspects of dominant interpretation outlined above are questioned in the analysis which follows. Chapter 2 is a descriptive and exploratory chapter which sets out a detailed analysis of the forms and techniques of clearing bank regulation. While it slightly simplifies the regulatory landscape, for analytical purposes clearing bank regulation in the period is classified as assuming three forms: codified regulation in the form of primary or secondary legislation; extra-legal (or non-statutory) regulation; and self-regulation. This chapter also comments on the degree of compliance with regulation arguing that generally, it was high. The description and exploration of the nature of clearing bank regulation in Chapter 2 are followed by a discussion in Chapter 3 of the context within which the clearing banks operated and were regulated, the rationale behind the authorities' approach to regulation, and some of the consequences of the approach. Two aspects of the context are considered: the economic context and the industry context—the structure of the banking industry. It then examines the rationale behind the regulatory framework and questions the extent to which it was motivated by the policy of financial repression. The final section of Chapter 3 explores the claim that the approach taken to bank regulation had unanticipated consequences in that its strong focus on the regulation of the London clearing banks led to other areas being too lightly or even unregulated and that the existence of these unregulated sectors contributed to the secondary banking crisis. Chapter 4 turns to bank regulation today and identifies some keys points of contrast between the approach to bank regulation in the period under review and that taken since the global financial crisis 2007–2009. Chapter 5 makes some concluding comments about the context in the earlier period and offers two points for reflection for banks, regulators and regulatory policymakers.

Any references in the text to ""the Bank" are references to the Bank of England.

Notes

1. The London clearing banks operated mainly in England and Wales, and to a lesser degree in Northern Ireland. The Scottish banks (which are outside the scope of this study) operated as clearing banks in Scotland. In 1985 the CLCB and its counterpart in Scotland merged to form the Committee of London and Scottish Bankers, and in 1991 the new Committee was subsumed into the broader British Bankers' Association.
2. Mae Baker and Michael Collins, "London as an International Banking Center, 1950–1980," in *London and Paris as International Financial Centres in the Twentieth Century*, ed. Youssef Cassis and Eric Bussière, Oxford Scholarship Online (Oxford: Oxford University Press, 2007): 2–3.
3. See David K. Sheppard, *The Growth and Role of UK Financial Institutions, 1880–1962* (London and New York: Routledge, 2006): Table (A) 1.6 and Table (A) 1.8.
4. Committee to Review the Functioning of Financial Institutions, *Report*, Cmnd. 7937, June 1980, Appendix 10, Table 10.8. By 1978 the clearing banks' share of such lending had reduced to 39%, although the amount of lending by the banking sector had increased by then to £50 billion: ibid.
5. Carmen M. Reinhart and Kenneth S. Rogoff, *This Time Is Different: Eight Centuries of Financial Folly* (Princeton: Princeton University Press, 2009): 205.
6. Richard S. Grossman, "Banking Crises," *Wesleyan Economic Working Papers* 2016-001 (May 2016): Section 6, accessed 13 July 2018, http://repec.wesleyan.edu. Grossman refers to this period as "the Great Lockdown," redolent of the description of it as a period of "financial repression."
7. "Global Finance After the Crisis," Alan M. Taylor, *Bank of England Quarterly Bulletin* (Quarter 4, 2010): 371, accessed 12 July 2018, https://www.bankofengland.co.uk/quarterly-bulletin/2010/q4/global-finance-after-the-crisis.

8. Kobrak and Troege examine these failures in the context of their exploration of the origin and evolution of the Basel Accords. Christopher Kobrak and Michael Troege, "From Basel to Bailouts: Forty Years of International Attempts to Bolster Bank Safety," *Financial History Review* 22, no. 2 (2015). The Committee had been established in 1974 as the Committee on Banking Regulations and Supervisory Practices by the governors of the central banks of the Group of Ten (G10) countries. "History of the Basel Committee," *Bank for International Settlements*, accessed 14 July 2018, https://www.bis.org/bcbs/history.htm. Schenk also explores the approach of the Basel Committee on Banking Supervision at its origins: Catherine R. Schenk, "Summer in the City: Banking Failures of 1974 and the Development of International Banking Supervision," *English Historical Review* CXXIX, no. 540 (2014): 1141–45.
9. Michael D. Bordo and Christopher M. Meissner, "Fiscal and Financial Crises," *Handbook of Macroeconomics Vol. 2 Conference* (9–11 April 2015): 13, accessed 17 June 2017, http://www.hoover.org/sites/default/files/bordo-meissner-north_holland_paper-4_hoover.pdf.
10. Forrest Capie and Mark Billings, "Evidence on Competition in English Commercial Banking, 1920–1970," *Financial History Review* 11, no. 1 (April 2004): 69.
11. Forrest Capie and Mark Billings, "Profitability in English Banking in the Twentieth Century," *European Review of Economic History* 5, no. 3 (2001): 367.
12. Robert Neild, "The National Debt in Perspective," *Royal Economic Society*, accessed 6 July 2018, http://www.res.org.uk/view/article5jan-12Correspondence.html. By 1970, the ratio was 67%.
13. Carmen M. Reinhart, Jacob F. Kirkegaard, and M. Belen Sbrancia, "Financial Repression Redux," *Finance and Development* 48, no. 1 (June 2011): 22, accessed 26 October 2017, http://www.imf.org/external/pubs/ft/fandd/2011/06/pdf/reinhart.pdf.
14. Tansey and Jackson cite Graham T. Allison (1987) as the source of this model. See Stephen D. Tansey and Nigel Jackson, *Politics: The Basics*, 4th ed. (Abingdon: Routledge, 2008): 222.
15. John Turner, *Banking in Crisis: The Rise and Fall of British Banking Stability, 1800 to the Present* (Cambridge: Cambridge University Press, 2014): 181, 186.
16. William A. Allen, *Monetary Policy and Financial Repression in Britain, 1951–59* (Basingstoke: Palgrave Macmillan, 2014): 240.
17. James Reveley and John Singleton, "Clearing the Cupboard: The Role of Public Relations in London Clearing Banks' Collective Legitimacy-Seeking, 1950–1980," *Enterprise and Society* 15, no. 3 (2014): 474, 476.

18. Duncan Needham, *UK Monetary Policy from Devaluation to Thatcher, 1967–82* (Basingstoke: Palgrave Macmillan, 2014): 14.
19. Ranald C. Michie, "Chapter 6: Control and Compartmentalization, 1945–1970," in *British Banking: Continuity and Change from 1694 to the Present* (Oxford: Oxford University Press, 2016): 184, 182.
20. Grossman, "Banking Crises": Section 6.
21. Margaret Ackrill and Leslie Hannah, *Barclays: The Business of Banking 1690–1996* (Cambridge: Cambridge University Press, 2001): ix.
22. Ibid., 204.
23. Mae Baker and Michael Collins, "English Commercial Banks and Organizational Inertia: The Financing of SMEs, 1944–1960," *Enterprise & Society* 11, no. 1 (March 2010): 66–68, accessed 5 May 2016, https://muse.jhu.edu/article/375590.
24. Ibid., 68.
25. Paul Thompson, "The Pyrrhic Victory of Gentlemanly Capitalism: The Financial Elite of the City of London, 1945–90," *Journal of Contemporary History* 32, no. 3 (July 1997): 290.
26. Duncan McDougall Ross, *The Clearing Banks and the Finance of British Industry, 1930–1959* (PhD thesis, London School of Economic and Political Science, 1989): 257, accessed 13 July 2018, British Library Ethos e-theses online service.
27. Glyn Davies, *A History of Money*, 3rd ed. (Cardiff: University of Wales Press, 2002; reprint, 2010): 422–23. Under the liability management model, rather than the starting point for a bank's lending strategy being its deposit base, the starting point instead would be the demand for loans. The bank would then determine how to fund that level of demand for loans by actively managing (i.e. increasing or decreasing) the level of its deposits which, from the bank's point of view, are liabilities on its Balance Sheet.
28. Bernardo Bátiz-Lazo and Peter Wardley, "Banking on Change: Information Systems and Technologies in UK High Street Banking, 1919–1969," *Financial History Review* 14, no. 2 (2007): 180–81. See also: Bernardo Bátiz-Lazo, "Emergence and Evolution of ATM Networks in the UK, 1967–2000," *Business History* 51, no. 1 (2009).
29. Michael Collins and Mae Baker, "English Bank Business Loans, 1920–1968: Transaction Bank Characteristics and Small Firm Discrimination," *Financial History Review* 12, no. 2 (2005): Table 3.
30. Ibid., 167.
31. Francesca Carnevali, *Europe's Advantage: Banks and Small Firms in Britain, France, Germany, and Italy Since 1918* (Oxford: Oxford University Press, 2005): 25.

32. Duncan McDougall Ross, *The Clearing Banks and the Finance of British Industry, 1930–1959* (PhD thesis, London School of Economic and Political Science, 1989): 86–93, accessed 13 July 2018, British Library Ethos e-theses online service. Ross uses a case study of the firm Babcock and Wilcox over the period 1930–1959 to illustrate the sometimes long-term nature of bank advances.
33. Ibid., 2, 93.
34. Geoffrey Ingham, *Capitalism Divided? The City and Industry in British Social Development* (Basingstoke: Macmillan Education Ltd., 1984): 134.

References

Primary Sources

Command Papers

Committee to Review the Functioning of Financial Institutions, *Report*, Cmnd. 7937, June 1980.

Secondary Sources

Theses

Ross, Duncan McDougall. "The Clearing Banks and the Finance of British Industry, 1930–1959." PhD thesis, London School of Economics and Political Science, 1989. Accessed 13 July 2018. British Library Ethos e-theses online service.

Books and Articles

Ackrill, Margaret, and Leslie Hannah. *Barclays: The Business of Banking 1690–1996*. Cambridge: Cambridge University Press, 2001.

Allen, William A. *Monetary Policy and Financial Repression in Britain, 1951–59*. Basingstoke: Palgrave Macmillan, 2014.

Baker, Mae, and Michael Collins. "London as an International Banking Center, 1950–1980." In *London and Paris as International Financial Centres in the Twentieth Century*, edited by Youssef Cassis and Eric Bussière, 1–23. Oxford: Oxford University Press, 2007. Accessed 15 February 2014. http://www.oxfordscholarship.com/view/10.1093/acprof:oso/9780199269495.001.0001/acprof-9780199269495-chapter-12.

Baker, Mae, and Michael Collins. "English Commercial Banks and Organizational Inertia: The Financing of SMEs, 1944–1960." *Enterprise & Society* 11, no. 1 (March 2010): 65–97. Accessed 5 May 2016. https://muse.jhu.edu/article/375590.

Bátiz-Lazo, Bernardo. "Emergence and Evolution of ATM Networks in the UK, 1967–2000." *Business History* 51, no. 1 (2009): 1–27.

Bátiz-Lazo, Bernardo, and Peter Wardley. "Banking on Change: Information Systems and Technologies in UK High Street Banking, 1919–1969." *Financial History Review* 14, no. 2 (2007): 177–205.

Bordo, Michael D., and Christopher M. Meissner. "Fiscal and Financial Crises." *Handbook of Macroeconomics Vol. 2 Conference* (9–11 April 2015). Accessed 17 June 2017. http://www.hoover.org/sites/default/files/bordo-meissner-north_holland_paper-4_hoover.pdf.

Capie, Forrest, and Mark Billings. "Profitability in English Banking in the Twentieth Century." *European Review of Economic History* 5, no. 3 (2001): 367–401.

Capie, Forrest, and Mark Billings. "Evidence on Competition in English Commercial Banking, 1920–1970." *Financial History Review* 11, no. 1 (April 2004): 69–103.

Carnevali, Francesca. *Europe's Advantage: Banks and Small Firms in Britain, France, Germany, and Italy Since 1918*. Oxford: Oxford University Press, 2005.

Collins, Michael, and Mae Baker. "English Bank Business Loans, 1920–1968: Transaction Bank Characteristics and Small Firm Discrimination." *Financial History Review* 12, no. 2 (2005): 135–71.

Davies, Glyn. *A History of Money*. 3rd ed. Cardiff: University of Wales Press, 2002. Reprint, 2010.

Grossman, Richard S. "Banking Crises." *Wesleyan Economic Working Papers* 2016-001 (May 2016). Accessed 13 July 2018. http://repec.wesleyan.edu.

Ingham, Geoffrey. *Capitalism Divided? The City and Industry in British Social Development*. Basingstoke: Macmillan Education Ltd., 1984.

Kobrak, Christopher, and Michael Troege. "From Basel to Bailouts: Forty Years of International Attempts to Bolster Bank Safety." *Financial History Review* 22, no. 2 (2015): 133–56.

Michie, Ranald C. "Chapter 6: Control and Compartmentalization, 1945–1970." In *British Banking: Continuity and Change from 1694 to the Present*, 162–93. Oxford: Oxford University Press, 2016.

Needham, Duncan. *UK Monetary Policy from Devaluation to Thatcher, 1967–82*. Basingstoke: Palgrave Macmillan, 2014.

Reinhart, Carmen M., and Kenneth S. Rogoff. *This Time Is Different: Eight Centuries of Financial Folly*. Princeton: Princeton University Press, 2009.

Reinhart, Carmen M., Jacob F. Kirkegaard, and M. Belen Sbrancia. "Financial Repression Redux." *Finance and Development* 48, no. 1 (June 2011). Accessed 26 October 2017. http://www.imf.org/external/pubs/ft/fandd/2011/06/pdf/reinhart.pdf.

Reveley, James, and John Singleton. "Clearing the Cupboard: The Role of Public Relations in London Clearing Banks' Collective Legitimacy-Seeking, 1950–1980." *Enterprise and Society* 15, no. 3 (2014): 472–98.

Schenk, Catherine R. "Summer in the City: Banking Failures of 1974 and the Development of International Banking Supervision." *English Historical Review* CXXIX, no. 540 (2014): 1129–56.

Sheppard, David K. *The Growth and Role of UK Financial Institutions, 1880–1962*. London and New York: Routledge, 2006.

Tansey, Stephen D., and Nigel Jackson. *Politics: The Basics*. 4th ed. Abingdon: Routledge, 2008.

Thompson, Paul. "The Pyrrhic Victory of Gentlemanly Capitalism: The Financial Elite of the City of London, 1945–90." *Journal of Contemporary History* 32, no. 3 (July 1997): 283–304.

Turner, John. *Banking in Crisis: The Rise and Fall of British Banking Stability, 1800 to the Present*. Cambridge: Cambridge University Press, 2014.

CHAPTER 2

The Nature of Clearing Bank Regulation

Abstract This chapter describes and explores the nature of clearing bank regulation in the period from 1946 until the early 1970s. For analytical purposes, it classifies regulation as taking the form of codified regulation, normally in the form of primary legislation; extra-legal regulation (that is, non-statutory regulation, or "soft law"); and self-regulation. It begins by briefly summarizing the legal framework within which the clearing banks operated. It then explores the non-statutory ways in which the banks were regulated, including ratio requirements, deposits schemes, quantitative and qualitative guidance on lending, the provision of information and moral suasion. It also considers the constraints over the activities of the clearing banks which regulated them indirectly. It closes by considering the self-regulatory aspects of clearing bank regulation.

Keywords Cash ratio · Liquidity ratio · Special Deposits Scheme · Moral suasion · Codified regulation · Extra-legal regulation · Self-regulation

As the primary purpose of this chapter is to describe and explore the nature of clearing bank regulation, it is useful at the outset to reflect upon the meaning of the term regulation itself. Orbach proposes a broad definition stating that, "For all practical purposes, regulation [...] means intervention in the private domain."[1] Selznick posits regulation as the

© The Author(s) 2018

L. Arch, *The Regulation of the London Clearing Banks, 1946–1971*, Palgrave Studies in Economic History,
https://doi.org/10.1007/978-3-030-00910-6_2

"sustained and focused control exercised by a public agency over activities that are valued by a community" adding that the regulated activity is one which is "worthwhile in itself."[2] Black puts forward a definition of regulation as "the intentional activity of attempting to control, order, or influence the behaviour of others" while suggesting that an alternative more purposive definition might be "the sustained and focused attempt to alter the behaviour of others according to defined standards or purposes with the intention of producing a broadly defined outcome or outcomes."[3] It should be noted that while intervention is most commonly thought of as a "control or constraint," regulation also "enables, facilitates, or adjusts activities, with no restrictions."[4] This process of controlling, ordering or influencing the behaviour of the London clearing banks in the period under review took several forms and these are considered next.

2.1 Codified Regulation

Regulation in its most codified, formal and explicit guise took the form of legislation and is a useful starting point for considering the nature of clearing bank regulation. The legal framework governing banking as it developed over the twentieth century until the Banking Act 1979 is set out below. As will be seen, four bodies had a regulatory and/or supervisory role of some kind within this framework: the Bank of England, the Board of the Inland Revenue, the Board of Trade and HM Treasury.

2.1.1 Moneylenders Acts 1900–1927

The 1900 Act required moneylenders to be registered but was significant in that it drew a distinction between moneylending and banking. Those carrying on the business of banking were exempt from the registration requirement. The Act provided that "no moneylender may be registered under that Act by any name including the word 'bank,' or suggesting that he carries on the business of banking."[5] From 1967, under Section 123 of that year's Companies Act, banks could apply to the Board of Trade for a certificate of exemption from the provisions of the Moneylenders Acts on the grounds were carrying on the business of banking, rather than their status as a bank being decided by the courts.

2.1.2 Companies Act 1929, Sections 131 (I) and 358

This Act set out certain company registration and external reporting requirements for banks. Under Section 131 (I) of the Act:

> A limited banking company must, before it commences business, and also on the first Monday in February and the first Tuesday in August every year, make a statement in the Form set out in the Seventh Schedule of the Act, giving the amount of the share capital, the number of shares into which it is divided, the number issued, the calls made and paid, and the liabilities and assets of the bank on the previous 1st January or 1st July. A copy of this statement must be put up in a conspicuous place in the registered office of the bank, and also in every branch office. Every member and every creditor of the company shall be entitled to a copy of the statement on payment of a sum not exceeding 6d.[6]

Section 358 required a bank to register when it reached a certain size: "no company, association, or partnership, consisting of more than ten persons, may be formed for the purpose of carrying on the business of banking, unless it is registered as a Company under the Act."[7]

2.1.3 Bank of England Act 1946

This Act defined the relationship between the Treasury and the Bank of England and also defined the regulatory relationship between the Bank of England and other banks. It defined the former as follows: "The Treasury may from time to time give such directions to the Bank as, after consultation with the Governor of the Bank, they think necessary in the public interest."[8] The relationship between the Bank and other banks was couched in similar terms: "The Bank, if they think it necessary in the public interest, may request information from and make recommendations to bankers, and may, if so authorised by the Treasury, issue directions to any banker for the purpose of securing that effect is given to any such request or recommendation."[9] In its report of August 1959, the Committee on the Working of the Monetary System—the Radcliffe Committee—observed that the wording of the Bank of England Act 1946 had not actually altered the relationship between the Bank of England and the clearing banks, it had simply formalized it. The relationship now enshrined in law was not substantively different from the relationship which had prevailed up to 1946. Moreover, the Committee noted that by 1959 the power of the Bank to issue directions to banks had never needed to be used.[10] It also pointed out that the Bank's relationship with clearing banks was a regulatory and not a supervisory one, observing that "The Bank of England does not formally inspect or supervise the policies or operations of the clearing banks."[11] Although the terms "macro-prudential" and "micro-prudential" were not in use at the time, this suggests that the Bank's concern was macro-prudential, being concerned with the banking system as a whole, rather than micro-prudential and thus concerned with the detailed supervision of individual banks.

2.1.4 Exchange Control Act 1947

Under this Act, institutions could be authorized by the Treasury to deal in gold and foreign exchange and could open accounts for non-residents. These institutions were known as the "authorised banks."[12] Authorization under the Exchange Control Act 1947 signified a bank of the highest possible status.[13] It was normally only granted to banks in the primary banking sector. Branches of foreign banks were subject to the same authorization process as domestic banks. The list of authorized banks under the Exchange Control Act was more extensive than the list of Companies Act 1948 Schedule VIII banks described below.

2.1.5 Companies Act 1948, Schedule VIII

This Act provided for institutions recognized as banking or discount companies by the Board of Trade to be given certain exemptions with respect to the content of their annual accounts. Institutions with such recognition were sometimes referred to as the "Schedule eight" banks. Recognition was only granted to primary banking sector banks. The 1948 Act had its origins in the report of a Committee on Company Law Amendment—the Cohen Committee—appointed in June 1943 to "consider and report what major amendments are desirable in the Companies Act, 1929, and, in particular, to review the requirements prescribed in regard to the formation and affairs of companies and the safeguards afforded for investors and for the public interest."[14] The Committee had recommended that banking and discount companies should be exempt from various disclosure requirements with respect to their Balance Sheet and Profit and Loss Account. For example, they were not required to disclose the market value of certain investments—these investments could be shown in the Balance Sheet at historical cost. A less detailed Profit and Loss Account was required. In terms of defining to which companies these privileges should apply, it was sufficient that each company satisfied the Board of Trade that "it ought to be treated for the purposes of this Schedule [the Eighth Schedule] as a banking company or as a discount company."[15] As at March 1961, according to the Report of the Company Law Committee, there were 107 banking or discount companies on the Board of Trade's list.[16]

2.1.6 *Income Tax Act 1952, Section 200*

The Income Tax Act set out a further basis for defining a bank. Institutions were regarded as bona fide banks if tax relief could be claimed in respect of interest paid to the institution. Such recognition could be given to discount houses and members of the Stock Exchange, as well as to banks. From the Inland Revenue's point of view, as long as "the recipient of the gross interest was a wealthy and responsible body there was no danger that the Revenue would be done out of the tax on the interest."[17] The Inland Revenue "consulted" the Bank of England on applications for recognition under the Act. This Act thus provided a wide definition of a bank.

2.1.7 *Protection of Depositors Act 1963*

The 1963 Act represented the first step in statutory control over the soliciting of deposits. Banks on the Schedule eight list under the Companies Act 1948 were exempted from the general prohibition on advertising for deposits introduced under this Act. Advertising brought with it certain external reporting obligations, such as being required to file accounts with both the Board of Trade and companies' registry twice a year.[18] Under Section 127 of the Companies Act 1967, banks recognized by the Board of Trade as such were also exempted from the prohibition.

2.1.8 *Companies Act 1967, Section 123 and 127*

Under Section 123, a certificate given by the Board of Trade that they were satisfied that a person could be treated for the purposes of the Moneylenders Acts 1900–1927 as carrying on the business of banking was conclusive evidence that they were carrying on that business. Normally, certifications were granted only to primary banking sector banks. However, a number of fringe banks also came to be certificated under Section 123. Under Section 127, restrictions on advertising for deposits under the Protection of Depositors Act 1963 did not apply to those banking and discount companies which were recognized for that purpose by the Board of Trade.

2.1.9 Income and Corporation Taxes Act 1970, Section 54

Under Section 54 only a company which was recognized by the Inland Revenue as carrying on a bona fide banking business in the UK was authorized to pay annual interest gross on deposit accounts and to receive annual interest gross on advances to UK borrowers.

2.1.10 Banking Act 1979

In the wake of the secondary banking crisis which began in December 1973, a White Paper was issued in August 1976 titled *The Licensing and Supervision of Deposit-Taking Institutions.*[19] This in turn led to the Banking Act 1979 which "invested the Bank for the first time with a statutory responsibility for the supervision of deposit-taking institutions. That responsibility had up till then been carried out on the basis of custom and usage and the Bank's long-standing authority in the City."[20] It was also significant in that it introduced a completely new mandatory deposit protection fund for deposits with licensed deposit-takers and recognized banks.

In the context of the legal framework outlined above, it should be noted that the Bank, in its capacity as bank regulator, tended to resist a highly codified approach to regulation. In 1966, for example, it opposed a statutory definition of a bank on the grounds that "in the experience of the Bank of England, the most important factor was the experience, integrity and ability of the directors" in evaluating the quality of a bank.[21] These criteria did not lend themselves easily to codification. Even into the mid-1970s after the secondary banking crisis the governor remained "fundamentally opposed" to the concept of bringing the banks under a comprehensive statutory umbrella. He argued that this might undermine the strong propensity of banks to comply with the wishes of the Bank:

> If it were to appear to the banks that the Bank's supervisory role would in future be dependent on powers given in the new legislation rather than on its traditional relationship with them, there would be the danger, inherent in all legally regulated systems, that they would gradually become less willing to accept its requests and recommendations unreservedly but would start enquiring whether they fell within the limits laid down in legislation.[22]

In contrast with codified regulation in the UK today—which includes not only UK primary and secondary legislation but also European Union directives and regulations and the Basel Committee on Banking Supervision's Basel III framework—the function of codified clearing bank regulation in the earlier period was not that of providing detailed rules. Rather, it established an overarching regulatory framework through the Bank of England Act 1946 and established the privileges and exemptions to which banks were entitled, by virtue of being banks.[23] The absence of a statutory definition of a bank meant that there was the possibility of multiple versions of the regulatory perimeter, however. Codified regulation was however only one form of bank regulation during the period under review. Extra-legal and self-regulation played important roles in the regulatory framework and these forms of regulation are considered next.

2.2 Extra-Legal Regulation

In addition to binding legal obligations, the operations of the clearing banks were subject to what might be termed extra-legal (or non-statutory) regulation, or "soft law." These were those rules of conduct which sat beyond the sphere of precise, legally-binding and enforceable obligations—the sphere of "hard law."[24] An overview the different techniques of extra-legal regulation is set out in Fig. 2.1.

Ratios were a form of regulation which influenced the structure of a bank's balance sheet. It is a moot point whether the cash and liquidity ratios were extra-legal regulation emanating from the regulator, or techniques of self-regulation. Originally, they were adopted by convention by the banks and were thus self-regulatory by nature. On the other hand, they are sometimes referred to in the primary sources as external controls emanating from the regulatory authorities, and are therefore included in the category of extra-legal regulation, for the purposes of this book. Strictly speaking the cash and liquidity ratios can be regarded as

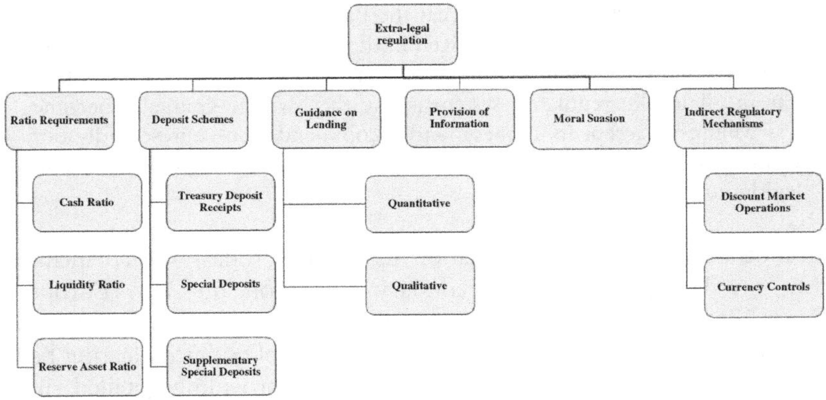

Fig. 2.1 Extra-legal regulation to the early 1970s

techniques which overlap both extra-legal and self-regulatory forms of regulation.

The cash ratio reflected the ratio of a bank's notes, coin and balances with the Bank of England (excluding Special Deposits) to its total deposits. As deposits made with a clearing bank are liabilities, the ratio reflected the percentage of its deposits that it would be able to repay immediately, if required, from assets held in the form of cash. The ratio acted as a control on lending because if a bank's deposit base grew (thereby expanding their capacity to lend) the existence of the cash ratio meant that they were required to maintain some of those new deposits in the form of notes, coin or balances with the Bank of England to maintain the ratio at the required level. The cash ratio was not codified in legislation but was a convention.

At the end of 1946 it was confirmed that the cash ratio would be a daily ratio of 8% rather than 10%.[25] The London clearing banks' compliance with this ratio is illustrated in Fig. 2.2. Towards the end of the period, there is evidence of slightly greater volatility in the ratio which may indicate that it was becoming more difficult to manage with the same precision as in the previous twenty years.

The importance of the cash ratio was reflected in the fact that it was the only ratio included in the "Monthly Statement of Balances of London Clearing Banks," the key report submitted by the CLCB to the Treasury. In money terms, as of January 1947 the eleven clearing banks

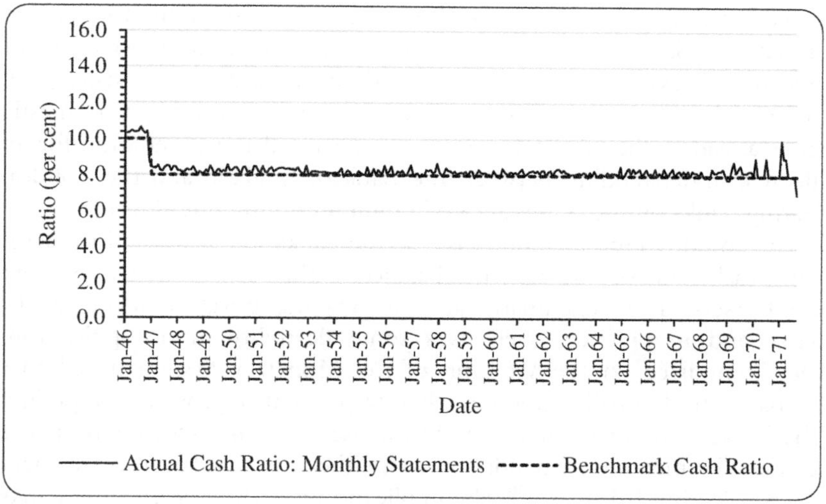

Fig. 2.2 Actual monthly cash ratio vs. benchmark cash ratio, January 1946–September 1971 (*Sources* (i) 1946–1966: "Monthly Statement of Balances of London Clearing Banks," LMA: CLC/B/029/MS32193/003-7; (ii) 1966–1971: *Bank of England Statistical Abstract Number 1, 1970, Table 9 (1)* and *Bank of England Statistical Abstract Number 2, 1975, Table 8/2*, accessed 24 July 2018, https://www.bankofengland.co.uk/-/media/boe/files/archive/statistical-abstract/number-1-1970.pdf and https://www.bankofengland.co.uk/-/media/boe/files/archive/statistical-abstract/number-2-1975.pdf)

held £475 million in aggregate in the form of notes, coin, bank notes and balances with the Bank of England and by January 1966 the figure stood at £758 million.[26] In September 1971 the cash ratio was dispensed with as part of the new policy of CCC.

The idea of a convention for bank liquidity had emerged in the wake of the bank failures of the nineteenth century. In 1885 the chair of the North and South Wales Bank advised in *The Country Banker* that, "To guard against all probable demands, therefore, I have put your immediately available resources [...] at one third the amount of your liabilities to the public [...]. Your reserve, therefore, should always be sufficient to meet every description of demand upon it."[27] By 1939 it was a firmly established banking convention that an amount equivalent to at least 30% of a bank's deposit liabilities should be held in the form of liquid assets.[28] The liquidity ratio was defined as shown in Fig. 2.3. As with the cash ratio, it had never been deemed necessary to codify the ratio in legislation: "Specific legislation in this form [of minimum ratios] has not appeared necessary in the United Kingdom because of the existence of a conventional pattern of assets structure to which the larger domestic banks already adhered. This convention provided the foundation for an informal understanding between the Bank of England and the London clearing banks on the observance of a minimum Liquidity Ratio."[29]

The liquidity ratio included cash, so the banks were expected to maintain a cash ratio of 8%, with the balance in the form of other specified liquid assets. The benchmark ratio of 30% was purely that—a benchmark—and in practice, there was some flexibility in its application. The Committee on the Working of the Monetary System noted that the banks traditionally adopted a highly prudent approach to liquidity: "the banks traditionally like to hold themselves in an exceedingly strong position for meeting demands for cash either for circulation or to meet adverse clearing balances."[30] The implication was that the clearing banks were, if anything, being over-prudent: the liquidity ratio "has been inherited from the period when the banks in this country were many more in number and much smaller in size."[31] By the time of the publication of the National Board for Prices and Incomes (NBPI) report on *Bank Charges* in May 1967, the liquidity ratio had settled at 28%.[32] Compliance with the liquidity ratio for the period 1946–1971 is illustrated in Fig. 2.4.

As can be seen, the liquidity ratio was subject to seasonal fluctuations. Liquid assets tended to fall between January and March because of annual payments of taxation. Liquidity, therefore, had to be built up between April and December in preparation.[33] As adherence to the liquidity ratio was conventional rather than statutory (as with the cash ratio), the Bank could only remonstrate with a bank if its ratio fell short of the benchmark. At a meeting with the chief executive officers (CEOs) in 1970 the Bank advised the CEOs that "one bank had fallen below 28% in liquidity in May [...] given that we had a system of ratios agreed

Numerator:	Coin, bank notes and balances with the Bank of England (excluding Special Deposits), money at call and short notice, UK treasury bills discounted, other bills discounted and re-financeable credits
Denominator:	Total deposits

Fig. 2.3 The liquidity ratio

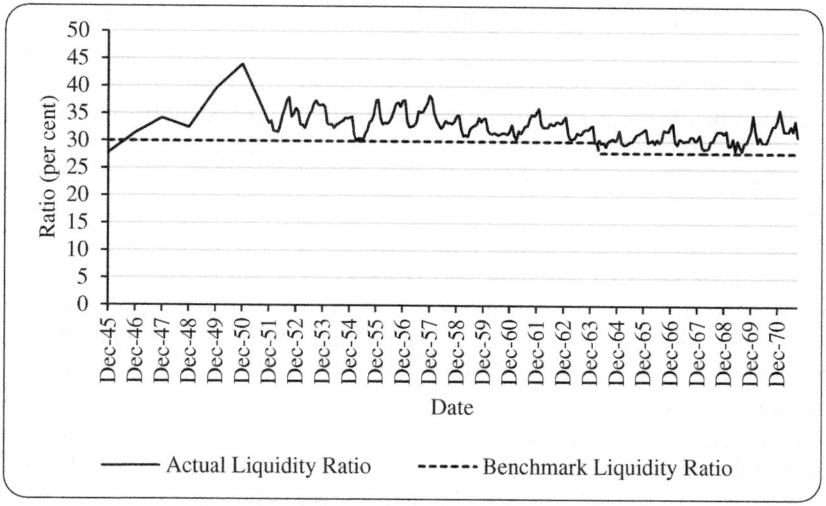

Fig. 2.4 Actual monthly liquidity ratio vs. benchmark liquidity ratio, December 1945–September 1971 (*Sources* (i) "Monthly Statement of Balances of London Clearing Banks," LMA CLC/B/029/MS32193/003-7; (ii) *Bank of England Statistical Abstract Number 1, 1970 Table 9 (1)* and *Bank of England Statistical Abstract Number 2, 1975, Table 8/2*, accessed 24 July 2018, https://www.bankofengland.co.uk/-/media/boe/files/archive/statistical-abstract/number-1-1970.pdf and https://www.bankofengland.co.uk/-/media/boe/files/archive/statistical-abstract/number-2-1975.pdf)

between the Bank and the banks, importance must be attached to their observance."[34] As with the cash ratio, the liquidity ratio was reported for the last time in September 1971, when the combined ratio for the six clearing banks as at 15 September 1971 stood at 30.7%.[35] The discontinuation of the cash and liquidity ratios can be seen as a strongly liberalizing measure, in that it lowered the barriers to entry into clearing banking. It also enabled the clearing banks to hold more of their assets in higher-yielding but riskier forms.

A growing problem with both the cash and liquidity ratios as regulatory techniques was the fact that they were adhered to by one part of the banking system only—the clearing banks. They were not applied to the growing number of overseas and other banks.[36] One of the far-reaching changes brought about by the policy of CCC in 1971 was that the cash and liquidity ratios were replaced by a single ratio, the reserve asset ratio or "reserve ratio" as it was often termed.[37] A key feature of CCC was that the reserve ratio would apply to *all* banks within the banking system not just the London clearing banks. Thus, the clearing banks, merchant banks, foreign banks in London, finance houses (with transitional arrangements) and certain bank subsidiaries were all covered by the new ratio requirement, although the savings banks, the National Giro and the building societies were outside its scope. The new ratio required banks to maintain an amount equivalent to at least 12.5% of their sterling term deposits of less than two years in the form of specified reserve assets. Reserve assets were defined as: balances with the Bank of England (other than Special Deposits or Supplementary Special Deposits), British government and Northern Ireland Treasury Bills, money at call with the London money market, company tax reserve certificates, British government securities with under one year to maturity, local authority bills and certain commercial bills. The ratio was to be observed daily. The new ratio would, argued the Bank, "provide the authorities with a known firm base for the operation of monetary policy."[38] On the eve of its introduction, the combined reserve ratio for five of the clearing banks stood at 16.2%, well above the required minimum under CCC of 12.5%.[39] In February 1973 the ratio for all banks stood at 14.6%.[40] This illustrates the clearing banks' prudence, in that they were holding considerably more reserve assets than was strictly required.

During the operation of the cash, liquidity and reserve asset ratios, another technique was used by the authorities to control the operations of clearing banks by influencing the structure of their balance sheets. This technique involved the placing of deposits directly with the Bank of England under a series of deposit schemes: Treasury Deposit Receipts (TDRs) (from 1940 until 1952), Special Deposits (from 1960 onwards) and the Supplementary Special Deposits Scheme (SSDS) which was activated on three occasions between 1973 and 1980. These schemes are explored in the next section.

Treasury Deposit Receipts had been introduced during the first year of the Second World War, on 1 July 1940. TDRs were loans from the banks held at the Bank of England, for the account of the Treasury. Their purpose was to place the funds that were accumulating in banks at the disposal of the government towards the war effort.[41] They represented the "surplus funds of bankers."[42] Loans of £92 million in the form of TDRs were recorded for the first time in September 1940.[43] By 31 March 1944 the amount had grown to £1389.5 million. The largest depositors were the London clearing banks (who accounted for £1292.5 million of the total), followed by the eight Scottish banks (£54 million) and two central banks, Australia and Egypt (£43 million).[44] Initially, interest payable on these deposits was at a rate of 1.125%. This was below the prevailing Bank Rate which, from 26 October 1939, had been 2%, at which level it would remain until 8 November 1951.[45] Unlike Treasury Bills, TDRs were not negotiable instruments. On the other hand, the rate payable on TDRs, although below the Bank Rate, was considerably higher than the Treasury Bill rate. The average rate on Treasury Bills from 1940 until 1945 was in the range 1.025–0.895%.[46] At its maximum in September 1945 over £2000 million was deposited with the Bank of England by the London clearing banks in the form of TDRs. Anxious to avoid any suggestion of profiteering during the war, the chair of Lloyds Bank drew attention in his statement to shareholders for the year ended 31 December 1946 to the low rate of interest earned by the bank on its liquid funds, including their TDRs. Their average earnings on their most liquid funds—cash, money at call, TDRs and Treasury Bills—was "below a half of one per cent" at a time when the Bank Rate was 2%.[47]

As at May 1947 TDRs had reduced to £1349.5 million but still represented 22.66% of the London clearing banks' combined assets.[48] TDRs continued to decline sharply over the next few years. At a meeting of the CLCB on 7 November 1951 the minutes recorded that "It is not the intention to abolish this method of finance, but it may not be utilised very much in the near future."[49] The last month in which an entry for Treasury Deposits Receipts was recorded in the Annual Abstract of Statistics was February 1952, when the amount was £20.8 million.[50] By 1953 no holdings of TDRs were shown in the "Monthly Statement of Balances of London Clearing Banks" and from October 1958 the item "Treasury Deposit Receipts" was no longer included in the monthly statement.[51]

From February 1952 until July 1958, control over the level and direction of clearing bank lending was exercised through a regime of requests by the Bank of England to the clearing banks. This practice ended temporarily in mid-1958, after the Bank was invited to prepare an alternative scheme to that regime. Accordingly, the Bank "armed itself with a new tool, 'special deposits'."[52] As with other techniques of extra-legal regulation, this new technique for controlling the banks was one which was not imposed upon them but was, as Dow points out, was "negotiated" with them.[53] The consultation paper issued by the Bank in May 1971, Competition and Credit Control, summarized Special Deposits thus: "The Special Deposits scheme provides for calls for deposits by the Bank of England to whatever extent the authorities deem necessary for the purposes of credit control and for payment of interest on such deposits close to the Treasury bill rate."[54] Special Deposits controlled bank lending because amounts placed on deposit with the Bank were not available for lending.

In June 1958 the Bank of England set out details of the scheme, stating that its overriding purpose was "to restrict the liquidity of the Banking system."[55] Special Deposits were called whenever it was deemed necessary "to control the lending of the banks."[56] The scheme was "accepted in principle" by the clearing banks at a meeting between the governor and the clearing bank chairs on 30 June.[57] The scheme provided for calls for Special Deposits to be made by the Court of the Bank of England in multiples of £100,000. The level of the call was a percentage of a bank's total gross deposits, based on the latest available monthly figure. Normally, if a call were made on a Thursday at that week's Court meeting the deposit was expected to be made at the Bank by the following Wednesday. For substantial calls a longer period would be permitted, sometimes spread over several weeks.[58] The banks would be paid interest of one-sixteenth above or below the average Treasury Bill tender rate for the preceding week, with the rate recalculated weekly. Banks could apply for releases from Special Deposits, but these "would not be lightly agreed to."[59] Special Deposits were not eligible for inclusion as liquid assets for the purpose of calculating the liquidity ratio and in 1958 the governor confirmed that the liquidity ratio of 30% would not be relaxed. The clearing banks were disappointed that the scheme was restricted to the London clearing banks and the Scottish banks, and did not apply to non-clearing banks or other financial institutions.

In parallel with the introduction of the new scheme, quantitative controls would lapse on 31 July 1958. From that date the total level of bank advances would not be restricted, with the chancellor announcing, "I need not ask the banks to restrict the total level of bank advances to any given figure after the end of July."[60] The guidance to the Capital Issues Committee (CIC) was also relaxed. Most notably, the threshold above which Treasury consent was required to raise new capital was increased from £10,000 (the threshold since March 1956) to £50,000.[61]

Why was it deemed necessary to develop and deploy the scheme of Special Deposits? At the Lord Mayor's Dinner in October 1958, the governor reflected on the advantages of the new scheme over the alternatives. Special Deposits were, he argued, "the most flexible, the most obviously 'monetary' in form and the least open to possible abuse as a method of inflationary borrowing by Government from the banking system."[62] This implied that quantitative controls over clearing bank lending were perceived as ineffective in controlling the rate at which the money supply grew. Special Deposits were flexible in that a call or a release of Special Deposits was logistically straightforward (calls and releases took place fairly frequently) and their effects more predictable than placing a ceiling on bank lending. Their principal purpose, the governor explained, was "to help in preventing excess liquidity from having its secondary effects in blowing up the credit balloon."[63] He described the way in which the scheme would operate to the Chancellor, Derick Heathcoat Amory, thus: "The scheme would serve to reinforce the existing monetary instruments and would be employed as a general control of credit in the same way and after the same sort of consideration as Bank Rate."[64] The introduction of Special Deposits can therefore be seen as adding to the monetary policy instruments available to the authorities in pursuit of monetary policy objectives to be deployed as required alongside other instruments of monetary policy. The amounts called over the period May 1960 to December 1979 are illustrated in Fig. 2.5. With the introduction of CCC in 1971, all banks were subject to Special Deposits, not just the London clearing banks.

Special Deposits operated alongside the liquidity ratio. As Special Deposits did not count as liquid assets, they would also not count in the calculation of banks' liquidity ratios. By requiring banks to place cash with the Bank of England, the banks' liquid assets would fall, as would their liquidity ratio. To restore the ratio to the required level of 30% they would need to either reduce their deposits or increase their liquid assets (by refraining from lending or by converting non-liquid assets into liquid ones). Except for the period between December 1963 and April 1965, numerous calls and releases of Special Deposits were made. By the late 1960s, however, the effectiveness of the technique began to be questioned. In his speech at the Lord Mayor's dinner in 1968 the governor suggested that Special Deposits were not necessarily effective in all circumstances. They might only be effective in regulating credit, he

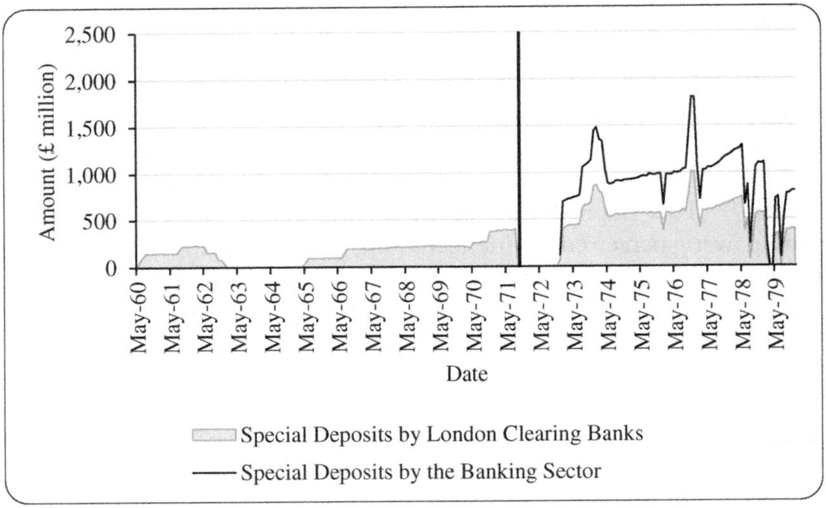

Fig. 2.5 Special deposits, May 1960–December 1979 (*Sources* (i) *Bank of England Statistical Abstract Number 1, 1970, Table 9 (1)* and *Bank of England Statistical Abstract Number 2, 1975, Table 8/2* and *9/3*, accessed 24 July 2018, https://www.bankofengland.co.uk/-/media/boe/files/archive/statistical-abstract/number-1-1970.pdf and https://www.bankofengland.co.uk/-/media/boe/files/archive/statistical-abstract/number-2-1975.pdf; (ii) *Bank of England Quarterly Bulletin* Quarter 4, 1974, 1975, 1976, 1977, 1978, and 1980, accessed 24 July 2018, https://www.bankofengland.co.uk/quarterly-bulletin/quarterly-bulletins; (iii) *Financial Statistics* Number 170, Table 35 (1976), Number 182, Table 6.1 (1977), Number 194, Table 6.1 (1978), Number 206, Table 6.1 (1979) and Number 218, Table 6.3 (1980), Central Statistical Office. *Notes* The new policy, Competition and Credit Control, was introduced in September 1971 as indicated by the vertical line. From May 1975, the figures for the London Clearing Banks include Supplementary Special Deposits)

implied, "when relatively mild control is all that is required."[65] The last call under the original Special Deposit Scheme was in December 1979.[66]

In its original guise the Special Deposits Scheme overlapped with a Supplementary Special Deposits Scheme which was first activated on 17 December 1973 as the secondary banking crisis broke. Although just beyond the period of this study, a brief description is provided. Goodhart credits Bank official Gilbert Wood as having coined the term "corset" for the SSDS. The scheme was a corset because it was "an external constraint to disguise and conceal internal flab."[67] Under the SSDS, banks were required to place deposits with the Bank of England if their interest-bearing eligible liabilities (IBELs) were growing faster than a specified rate. IBELs included interest-bearing sterling sight and time deposits of two years' maturity or less, net sterling deposits from other UK banks and certificates of deposit issued. The base figure used was each bank's average IBELs as at the August, September and October reporting dates. Growth was evaluated with reference to the current three-month moving average. If growth exceeded the guideline the bank was required to place a Supplementary Special Deposit with the Bank of England. No interest was payable by the Bank on these deposits. The aim of the corset was to put limits on the extent to which banks could expand their deposits, thereby discouraging them from bidding for funds in the wholesale money markets—markets which had grown rapidly in the wake of CCC. This would put downwards pressure on inter-bank and Certificate of Deposit rates. The SSDS was therefore seen as an alternative to increasing the Minimum Lending Rate directly. Supplementary Special Deposits were implemented on three occasions: from December 1973 to February 1975, from November 1976 to August 1977 and, finally, from June 1978 to June 1980.

As the number and importance of non-clearing banks grew, the government had to consider how to control the credit generated by these other institutions. In 1958, when the Special Deposit Scheme was conceived, non-clearing bank lending to the UK private sector was £200 million. By 1967 it had risen to £800 million.[68] Domestic deposits with the Accepting Houses amounted to £114 million in 1959, but £700 million in 1967. The equivalent figures for the overseas banks were even more spectacular: in 1959 they held resident deposits of £330 million and by the end of 1966 £1800 million.[69] The Bank had explicitly recognized by 1967 that "it is no longer possible to secure adequate control of lending by the banking sector generally through operating only on the clearing banks."[70] Accordingly, a scheme was developed by the Bank in collaboration with the non-clearing banks—the Cash Deposits Scheme—to address the issue. In the event, although formally the scheme was in operation from 1968, cash deposits were never called and the scheme was superseded by the reserve asset ratio requirement in 1971 under CCC.

Ackrill and Hannah describe the quantitative controls over lending as a regime of "rationing and 'requests'."[71] Quantitative restrictions on bank lending had been put in place during the Second World War, at the time of the introduction of TDRs on 1 July 1940. The governor requested all principal banks of the British Bankers' Association not to pay interest at a rate higher than 1% on either current or deposit accounts. The one exception was that banks retained some discretion over interest payable on the first £100 held in "Home Safe Accounts."[72]

There were five substantive iterations of quantitative controls and they appeared to have had a restraining effect on bank advances in their first, second and fourth iterations, but less so in their final iteration, even though they were by then being used in combination with calls for Special Deposits. It should also be borne in mind that bank lending in the UK traditionally took the form of overdraft lending rather than lending in the form of term loans. Consequently, it was always going to be difficult to control the aggregate level of clearing bank lending because the banks could not predict how much of their overdraft facility a customer would use. Quantitative controls were also politically problematic. They were a high-intensity form of bank regulation, redolent of wartime restrictions and controls. When quantitative controls were temporarily discontinued in July 1958, the Special Deposits Scheme was regarded as a much less intrusive technique of regulation and was deemed more appropriate to what was now a peacetime economy.

By the end of the 1960s, a strong argument could be made that quantitative controls were becoming less effective in controlling lending. On 18 June 1970 the Conservatives secured a thirty-seat majority at the general election, with 46.4% of the vote. The regime of direct quantitative controls over bank lending was decidedly out of step with the philosophy of the new government. In May 1971 the government proposed to end quantitative lending controls with its new policy of CCC. The argument was also being made that quantitative controls impeded the development of a genuinely competitive banking system. John Fforde's objection to direct quantitative controls was that they were damaging the legitimacy of the Bank.[73] His December 1970 paper asserted that the Bank's credibility was suffering because of six years of ceiling controls and that such policies were warping the very structure of the banking industry and the shape of the banking industry in the UK "should not be notably subordinated to the requirements of monetary policy."[74] Quantitative controls distorted the market and impeded the development of a level playing field—a prerequisite for competition in banking. The Bank also believed that the current approach was making the banking system *less* stable because it prevented the clearing banks from competing fully with, and ultimately eliminating, the inferior and less efficient fringe banks.[75] Capie argues that the single most important concern behind CCC was to increase competition in banking and to move away from direct controls over bank lending.[76]

The scope of quantitative guidance went beyond placing ceilings on clearing bank lending. It also controlled the provision of hire purchase finance. Initially, the clearing banks had become involved in hire purchase by providing finance to hire purchase companies. From the late 1950s the banks were permitted to participate in hire purchase companies by holding shares in them or by establishing hire purchase subsidiary companies.[77] The governor welcomed their participation: "I judge this closer connection between the banking system and the Hire Purchase industry to be in the public interest."[78] Hire purchase lending grew strongly into the 1960s and the involvement of the clearing banks was seen as a stabilizing influence in what was a relatively volatile part of the banking system. By 1969, 86% of finance houses that belonged to the Finance Houses Association were owned either wholly or substantially by one of the clearing banks.[79] Details of the quantitative guidance issued to the clearing banks in relation to the level and/or direction of their lending from 1952 to 1973 are set out in Table 2.1.

Qualitative guidance was also regulation which was extra-legal in nature. Qualitative guidance was concerned with the direction of bank lending rather than its level. Sometimes lending or investment was guided positively *towards* certain activities. Typically, this involved the chancellor communicating to the banking system via the Bank of England where it wished to see lending directed. Sometimes such guidance was broad (as with the guidance to direct lending to export-oriented industries). At other times, it was narrow (towards a specific industry, such as shipbuilding, or when the banks were encouraged to take shareholdings in finance agencies, such as the Industrial and Commercial Finance Company Ltd.). Qualitative guidance could also take the form of negative guidance, where banks were discouraged from lending to certain activities. Throughout the late 1940s and 1950s this applied to lending for speculation, for example. Qualitative guidance tended to focus on the following areas: exports and shipbuilding; finance agencies; capital issues and capital expenditure; and speculative activities.

From 1961 several schemes were put in place to encourage the clearing banks to lend for shipbuilding and/or exports.[80] The clearing banks funded both activities at low, fixed rates of interest (5.5% until 1973).

Table 2.1 Quantitative guidance to London clearing banks, 1952–1973

Date	*Quantitative guidance*
February 1952	Controls over hire purchase were introduced through The Minimum Deposits and Maximum Repayment Term (Board of Trade Order) under the Defence (General) Regulations, 1939. This specified minimum initial deposits (of 33.33%) and maximum repayment periods of 18 months for private motor vehicles, domestic appliances and radios and televisions. In tandem, the banks were guided to reduce their facilities to hire purchase companies by 10% initially and then by a further 10% after twelve months[a]
August 1954	The above restrictions were rescinded[b]
25 July 1955	The banks were given guidance that "It is their [the banks'] duty to reduce the amount of bank credit below what they would be glad to give in less difficult times."[c] Facilities to hire purchase companies were to be reduced by 10% by 31 October 1955 and by a further 5% by 31 December 1955.[d] This marked the beginning of the "credit squeeze." In June 1955, Lloyds advances covered by the guidance amounted to £298.5 million and by December 1956 stood at £278.4 million.[e] The Chair of Lloyds described in the Annual Report for 1955 how "The staff have had a harassing year. Upon our branch managers up and down the country and upon the officials at Head Office has fallen the task - a very onerous and distasteful task - of implementing the policy of credit restriction"[f]
19 September 1957	The banks were given guidance that "The average level of bank advances during the next twelve months should be held at the average level for the last twelve months"[g]
1 July 1958	The total level of advances was no longer restricted to any given figure after the end of July 1958[h]
1958–1960	The period from July 1958 to April 1960 was a period without lending restrictions
April 1960	Controls over hire purchase were reintroduced and the first call for Special Deposits was made.[i] A relaxation of hire purchase controls occurred in January 1961 when the maximum repayment period was extended to thirty-six months
25 July 1961	The clearing banks agreed to reduce the facilities given to hire purchase companies by at least 10% by October 1961 and by a further 10% by January 1962.[j] The clearing banks were also guided to "cut considerably the rate of increase in advances by the end of this year."[k] The guidance of the Conservative chancellor, Selwyn Lloyd, left room for interpretation, "He [the Chancellor] was not proposing to give any direction to the banks about what to do but he hoped that we should set our faces against personal and professional loans, hire-purchase finance and building or property development and in general speculative applications"[l]

(continued)

Table 2.1 (continued)

Date	*Quantitative guidance*
October 1962	Restrictions on lending were removed[m]
March 1965	A 105% credit ceiling was applied to overseas banks and Accepting Houses[n]
7 May 1965 and 28 June 1965	Members of the Finance Houses Association and Industrial Bankers' Association and other larger finance houses were requested to ensure that credit granted did not increase by more than around 5% for the period to March 1966. The guidance was subsequently extended beyond March 1966.[o] The clearing banks were requested to ensure that their advances by mid-March 1966 did not exceed 105% of the figure at mid-March 1965[p]
February 1966	The 105% limitation on clearing banks was "extended indefinitely" but in practice lasted until April 1967[q]
July 1966	Severe controls were introduced on hire purchase finance. Deposits on automobiles, for example, were increased to 40% with a repayment period of twenty-four months
11 April 1967	The ceiling on lending by the clearing banks to the private sector was discontinued. Lending by other banks and by finance houses continued to be restricted to 105% of the March 1965 figure[r]
November 1967	The banks were given guidance that "Lending for most purposes must be held down in aggregate to the current level." Fixed-rate lending for shipbuilding and exports was excluded[s]
23 May 1968	An advances ceiling of 104% of the November 1967 figure was imposed until November 1968. This time, finance for export and shipbuilding was included in the ceiling[t]
22 November 1968	A lending ceiling of 98% of the mid-November 1967 level was to be achieved by mid-March 1969. The ceiling excluded fixed-rate lending (such as for exports and shipbuilding). Other banks were requested to ensure that their lending did not exceed 102% of the mid-November 1967 level by the end of March 1969. The package of measures included an Import Deposit Scheme from 25 November whereby 50% of the value of the goods would have to be deposited with Customs before release, to be repaid after 180 days[u]
June 1969	The rate payable on Special Deposits was halved in response to clearing banks' failure to achieve the ceiling. It was restored the following April[v]
April 1970	London clearing banks and Scottish banks were requested to ensure that their lending did not increase by more than around 5% over the twelve months from mid-March 1970. The rate of growth by other banks was restricted to not more than a 7% increase. Members of the Finance Houses Association and other non-member finance houses were restricted to growth of not more than 5% with effect from 31 March 1970[w]

(continued)

Table 2.1 (continued)

Date	*Quantitative guidance*
August 1972	On 7 August, the banks were requested to "make credit less readily available to property companies and for financial transactions not associated with the maintenance and expansion of industry"[x]
September 1973	Banks were requested to pay no more than 9.5% on any deposit of less than £10,000. This applied to any new fixed rate deposits and to existing floating rate ones[y]

[a]i. Governor to the chairman of the Committee of London Clearing Bankers, "Hire Purchase Finance," 19 August 1954, LMA CLC/B/084/MS34844. ii. Meeting of the Chief Executive Officers of the Clearing Banks, 29 November 1951, LMA CLC/B/029/MS32037/007

[b]Governor to the chairman of the Committee of London Clearing Bankers, "Hire Purchase Finance," 19 August 1954, LMA CLC/B/084/MS34844

[c]Chancellor [R. A. Butler] to the Governor, 25 July 1955, LMA CLC/B/029/MS32259/002

[d]"Chief executive officers of clearing banks - Bankers' Advances," memorandum, 26 July 1955, LMA CLC/B/029/MS32259/002

[e]Lloyds Bank Limited Report and Accounts 1956, Statement by the Chairman (pages not numbered), LBGA HO/S/Rep/10

[f]Lloyds Bank Limited Report and Accounts 1955, Statement by the Chairman (pages not numbered), LBGA HO/S/Rep/10

[g]Chancellor [Peter Thorneycroft] to the Governor, 19 September 1957, LSE Piercy Collection 9/80: Capital Issues Committee

[h]Chancellor [Derick Heathcoat Amory] to the Governor, 1 July 1958, LMA CLC/B/029/MS32259/004

[i]Lloyds Bank Limited Report and Accounts 1960, 16, LBGA HO/S/Rep/11–13

[j]Minutes of a Special Meeting of the Chief Executive Officers, 1 June 1962, LMA CLC/B/029/MS32037/012

[k]Minutes of a Special Meeting of the Committee of London Clearing Bankers 26 July 1961, LMA CLC/B/029/MS32037/012

[l]"Bank of England," 24 July 1961, LMA CLC/B/029/MS32259/005

[m]Winton, *Lloyds Bank, 1918–1969*, 175

[n]Note, 14 June 1968, TNA T326/793: Financial Control of Overseas Banks and Accepting Houses in the United Kingdom

[o]"Credit Restraint: Finance Houses' Statistics," 25 April 1966, BoE 6A127/1: Economic Intelligence Department: Hire Purchase

[p]Lloyds Bank Limited Report and Accounts 1965, Statement by the Chairman, 15, LBGA HO/S/Rep/14

[q]Lloyds Bank Limited Report and Accounts 1966, Statement by the Chairman, 19, LBGA HO/S/Rep/15–19

[r]"Credit Restraint 1967/68," notice, 11 April 1967, LMA CLC/B/029/MS 32259/006

[s]"Credit Restriction: New Measures, November 1967," *Bank of England Quarterly Bulletin* (Quarter 4, 1967): 348, accessed 26 July 2018, https://www.bankofengland.co.uk/quarterly-bulletin/1967/q4/credit-restriction—new-measures-november-1967

[t]Lloyds Bank Limited Report and Accounts 1968, Statement by the Chairman, 19–20, LBGA HO/S/Rep/15–19. Special Meeting of the Committee of London Clearing Bankers, 31 May 1968, LMA CLC/B/029/MS 32259/006

Table 2.1 (continued)

[u]"Credit Restriction," Bank of England Quarterly Bulletin (Quarter 4, 1968): 358-59, accessed 26 July 2018, https://www.bankofengland.co.uk/-/media/boe/files/quarterly-bulletin/1968/credit-restrictions-and-import-deposit-scheme-22-nov-1968

[v]Winton, *Lloyds Bank, 1918–1969*, 176, footnote 7

[w]"Notice: Bank and Finance House Lending 1970/71," 14 April 1970, BoE 8A180/1: Committee of London Clearing Bankers (CLCB) Chief Executive Officers—Minutes of Monthly Meetings

[x]"Bank Lending," *Bank of England Quarterly Bulletin* (Quarter 3, 1972): 327, accessed 25 July 2018, https://www.bankofengland.co.uk/quarterly-bulletin/1972/q3/bank-lending—the-governors-letter-to-the-banking-system-7-aug-1972

[y]"Credit Notice," *Bank of England Quarterly Bulletin* (Quarter 4, 1973): 445, accessed 7 June 2016, https://www.bankofengland.co.uk/quarterly-bulletin/1973/q4/credit-notice—the-governors-letter-to-the-main-banking-associations-11-sep-1973.pdf

As financing of shipbuilding (and exports) tended to be medium-term, this type of lending represented a departure from the clearing banks' normal practice of providing short-term working capital. In 1968 the clearing banks lobbied the Bank to increase the rate to 6% for funding up to five years, and to 7% for funding over five years. Longer term, they wished to be compensated by the authorities for the difference between the fixed rate they charged and the Bank Rate. The Bank was sensitive to the discrepancy between the Bank Rate and the rate for export finance. When the new lending ceiling was implemented in November 1968 the Bank agreed that the banks could exclude this category of lending when calculating the rates of growth in their lending. The Bank would not, however, agree to an increase in the fixed rate, their justification being the national interest: "in the national interest, no change could be made at present."[81] Subsequently, however, the fixed rates did increase, standing at 6% for export finance and 7% for shipbuilding by 1973.[82] By 1978 the minimum rate was 7.5% for shipbuilding lending and between 7.25 and 8% for export lending.[83] In terms of the scale of lending to exports and shipbuilding, as at December 1973 Lloyds' total export finance amounted to £627 million (including shipbuilding finance of £38 million), with a further £590 million agreed in principle. Approved and committed finance for shipbuilding amounted to £148 million.[84] In their evidence to the Wilson Committee in November 1977 the London clearing banks' lending for exports and shipbuilding under special schemes amounted to £2291 million, or 6.22% of their total sterling assets.[85]

In the post-war years the clearing banks were guided towards participation in various "special finance agencies." These agencies had been established over the course of the twentieth century, "with some level of official backing," to finance industry, trade and agriculture.[86] The principal ones were: the Industrial and Commercial Finance Corporation Ltd. (ICFC), which began operating on 20 July 1945; the Commonwealth Development Finance Co. Ltd.; the Finance Corporation for Industry Ltd. (authorized to begin operations on 19 May 1945); the Ship Mortgage Finance Corporation Ltd.; and the Agricultural Mortgage Corporation Ltd. Qualitative guidance took the form of the authorities' encouraging participation by the clearing banks in these agencies. This was not unique to the post-war period. The Agricultural Mortgage Corporation, for example, was a limited company set up in 1928 whose equity was owned by the Bank of England and nine joint-stock banks. The most important of these relationships after the war was between the ICFC and the clearing banks. The ICFC was formed in 1945 and was owned collectively by the Bank of England, the London clearing banks and the Scottish banks.[87] Coopey describes how "a series of plans and proposals were debated by Government departments [...] the Bank of England, the Clearing Banks and the Labour Party which eventually led to a decision in 1945 to establish two new institutions."[88] First, there was the ICFC whose purpose was to finance small and medium-sized businesses who required medium- (up to five years) and/or long-term capital, defined as between around £5000 and £200,000. Financing for larger amounts came under the remit of the second new institution, Finance Corporation for Industry. The work of the ICFC was meant to complement the work of the banks, rather than compete with them. It was not a bank per se and provided medium and long-term finance rather than overdraft facilities or revolving credit. Its share capital in the sum of £15 million was subscribed to by twenty clearing and Scottish banks, and the Bank of England. It did not have general borrowing powers and was only able to borrow from the subscribing banks.[89] To its chair, Lord Piercy, the ICFC had a special and distinctive role as a significant source of permanent capital to the private sector.[90] In 1959 the ICFC became a public company with the power to issue its own loan stock thus changing the relationship between the ICFC and the clearing banks.

Just as qualitative guidance could steer bank lending *towards* certain industries or activities, it could also steer lending away from those areas in which access to finance needed to be controlled or even prohibited. Typically, these were areas that might have an adverse impact upon the balance of payments by encouraging imports or by diverting investment away from export-oriented industries. The issue of new capital by a firm was one such area and was subject to strict controls. New capital issues came under the purview of the CIC. The CIC had been formally constituted in 1940 to ensure that new issues of capital were severely restricted unless they directly supported the war effort.[91] It approved or rejected applications for new issues of capital in accordance with government guidance. New issues were to be prioritized "according to their relative importance in the general national interest, having regard, particularly, to current Government policy in respect of physical investment."[92] As far as the London clearing banks were concerned, any lending for capital purposes was also expected to conform with the guidance to the CIC, which meant prioritizing lending for exports, undertakings in "Development Areas" and the exploitation or production of raw materials.[93] After the war, the Labour Chancellor of the Exchequer Sir Stafford Cripps issued a Special Memorandum decreeing that capital expenditure should be postponed unless it led directly or indirectly to "increasing exports or saving imports [...] or is of importance to such basic industries as agriculture, coal and steel production."[94] The Special Memorandum suggested that the total demand for manpower, steel, coal and other materials had to be reduced in order to meet the requirements of "the export industries and other vital purposes" for those resources.[95] There was also a quantitative dimension: the threshold above which Treasury consent was required to raise new capital was £50,000. The CIC became less active after 1959 and in November 1967 was formally dissolved.[96]

Speculation was another area subject to qualitative guidance. In the years after the war the clearing banks were explicitly guided not to lend for speculative purposes. Speculation in this context consists in buying and selling an item or asset to profit from a rise or fall in its market value, in contrast to buying and selling an item or asset for trade or investment purposes. In the aftermath of the Second World War it was the accepted custom that banks did not lend for speculative purposes. Qualitative guidance in relation to speculation took the form of requests from the Chancellor of the Exchequer to the clearing banks. In May 1945 the Chancellor Sir John Anderson called upon the banks to see that "no facilities should be given for the speculative buying or holding either of securities or stocks of commodities."[97] This guidance was reiterated two years later: "No facilities should be given for the speculative buying or holding of securities, real property or stocks of commodities; and that finance for hire purchase, particularly of consumer goods, should not be increased."[98] The need for strict controls was reiterated in April 1949 and again in 1951 and, on both occasions, the prohibition of lending for speculation was confirmed. In 1958, even though lending restrictions generally were lifted, those relating to speculation were not. In his letter to Lord Kennet, the chair of the CIC, the Conservative Chancellor Derick Heathcoat Amory confirmed that "consent for borrowing intended to finance the speculative buying or holding of shares, materials or real property (including the development of land) should continue to be withheld."[99] By July 1961 the wording of the chancellor's request in relation to lending for speculation had become rather less emphatic. The governor explained that "he [the Chancellor] hoped that we should set our faces against [...] speculative applications."[100] After this, explicit references to the prohibition of speculative lending in chancellors' requests ceased. In September of 1962, on the occasion of a release of Special Deposits back to the banks, there were no references to any restrictions on lending for speculation: "the Banks are free to lend again," as the *Times* put it.[101]

An important technique for regulating an industry is to require it to submit information on its activities to a regulatory body or bodies. Ogus suggests that regulation can be analysed according to the intensity of the regulatory intervention.[102] At one end of the spectrum, the high-intensity end, lies "prior approval" meaning that the regulated entity cannot undertake an activity without prior approval (as is normally the case with banking). At the other end of the spectrum lie lower intensity interventions such as the provision of information to the regulator. The requirement to submit information to a regulator was thus a low-intensity form of regulatory intervention in the clearing banking system. One aspect of the provision of information was the requirement for banks to publish annual accounts. The requirement to submit information to the regulator extended beyond the preparation and publication of financial statements and when the District Bank became a member of the Bankers' Clearing House in 1935 one of the criteria for membership was that it would publish a "Monthly Statement of Average Weekly Balances." Winton suggests that the London clearing banks started to publish these monthly statements in 1921.[103] This report was the centrepiece of London clearing bank reporting for many decades. The report of the

Table 2.2 Format of monthly statement of balances of London clearing banks, January 1966

Assets
Coin, bank notes and balances with the Bank of England
Balances with and cheques in course of collection on other banks in UK and Republic of Ireland
Money at call and short notice
Treasury Bills discounted
Other bills discounted and re-financeable credits
Special Deposits with the Bank of England
Investments at book value
Investments in affiliated banks and subsidiary companies
Advances to customers and other accounts
Bank premises account
Liabilities of customers and others for acceptances, endorsements, etc.
Total
Ratio of cash to current, deposit and other accounts
Liabilities
Capital paid up
Reserve fund
Current, deposit and other accounts
Acceptances, endorsements, etc.
Notes in circulation
Total

Source "Monthly Statement of Balances of London Clearing Banks," January 1966, LMA CLC/B/029/MS32193/007 (1964–1966)

Radcliffe Committee in 1959 observed that the monthly statements were not confidential, but in the public domain. They were made available to the press, as well as to the Treasury. A commentary on the monthly statement was also presented to the chancellor.[104] In contrast, it observed that the Scottish banks and discount houses supplied monthly figures to the authorities only and that, in addition, "Many of the accepting houses and merchant banks do not even publish balance sheets."[105] The format of the monthly statement, from 1966, is shown in Table 2.2.

By the mid-1970s, in the wake of CCC and the introduction of the Supplementary Special Deposit Scheme, three tables of information were being provided on a monthly basis: a table of "Aggregate Balances" which provided information similar to the previous monthly statement, but in more detail; a table of "Individual Groups of Banks' Balances"; and a table of "Credit Control Information."[106] These latter two tables covered the Big Four and Williams and Glyn's, and included aggregated figures. The third table reported on banks' reserve ratios, the ratio introduced as part of CCC.

The final technique of direct extra-legal regulation discussed here is moral suasion. What was meant by the term moral suasion? In Turner's analysis of why banks complied with Bank of England requests and directives, one of the reasons highlighted was "the Bank's power of moral suasion."[107] Moral suasion can be seen as the least interventionist form of extra-legal regulation. It was not a separate technique per se but was the foundation for extra-legal regulation in its entirety. Moral suasion underpinned each Bank request, directive or piece of guidance and compliance with these was witness to the Bank's power of moral suasion. Attard, in the context of the 1920s, suggests that moral suasion was the "typical way in which the Bank exercised its influence in the City, where the high degree of concentration, primacy of personal contacts and dependence on the Bank's goodwill made it [moral suasion] uniquely effective."[108] Busch emphasizes the immense extra-legal authority of the Bank, pointing out that this extended to the person of the governor: "The Bank's authority over the banking industry [...] did not emanate from legal regulations, but from the central role it played in the 'club-like' culture of the City, where the 'raised eyebrows' of its Governor were the ultimate sanction that would be strictly followed by everyone."[109] As an official put it, "The Bank's influence depends not on legislative sanctions but on authority established over time."[110] On *The Money Programme* in 1976, the chair of Lloyds Bank Sir Eric Faulkner opined that although it was fashionable "to mock at moral suasion," the latter was preferable to "some closely codified set of rules."[111] Schooner and Taylor characterize the newly nationalized Bank of England's power thus: "It influenced the process of credit creation through its powers of 'moral suasion'—the informal influence resulting from its long-standing relationship with the leading commercial banks."[112]

The significance of moral suasion within the regulatory framework was that it implied that the Bank of England was legitimate. Boulding argues that the gaining and maintaining of legitimacy is indispensable to a central bank, and indeed to institutions generally: "the dynamics of legitimacy," he argues, "is one of the most important elements in the total long-run dynamics of society [...] Its importance can be seen in the remark that if a person or institution loses legitimacy it loses everything.

It can no longer maintain itself in the social system. No amount of wealth, that is exchange capability, or power, that is, threat capability, can keep an institution alive if there is a widespread denial of the legitimacy of its role in society."[113] Being legitimate, the Bank's regulations had the quality of being binding. The London clearing banks felt duty-bound to adhere to requests, directives and guidance, even though they had no legal obligation to do so. It is worth reflecting that moral suasion had a characteristic which was quite unlike other forms or techniques of regulation: it was, by definition, wholly uncodified. Moral suasion was invisible, operating in the background. As Sayers put it in his book *Modern Banking*, "our Old Lady [the Bank of England] only gives curtain lectures."[114]

What was the significance of the Bank's reliance on extra-legal regulation? First, as a form of regulation its effectiveness depended upon the cooperation of the banks (and other institutions to whom it was directed) with the authorities and upon the willingness of the banks to comply with extra-legal regulation. It thus interwove the operations of the banks with the operations of the state. Second, it required and fostered cooperation *between* the banks, thus consolidating their tradition of cooperation with each other. When the clearing banks implemented official guidance they did so collectively. The Special Deposits Scheme, for example, was agreed by the clearing banks collectively through the CLCB. Cooperation in turn contributed towards the high degree of compliance with regulation. Third, it anchored the interests of the banks to the wider economy. For example, as shareholders of the ICFC, the clearing banks' interests were bound to those of small and medium businesses funded by the ICFC. Similarly, by lending for exports and shipbuilding their interests were intertwined with those sectors.

There were two other less direct constraints on banks which did not take the form of legislation or codified rules issued by the regulator, or of non-statutory regulation. First, there was the discount market and discount rates—the interest rates which prevailed in the Discount Market. In 1945, eleven discount houses with discount facilities at the Bank operated in that market. The discount houses intermediated between the Bank of England and the clearing banks and made a short-term money market. In contrast, by convention the clearing banks did not buy and sell Treasury Bills from the Bank directly and thus did not participate in that market. Instead, the clearing banks lent surplus cash to the discount houses by the day (at a collectively agreed rate and subject to suitable security from the discount house's own capital and reserves). Using these surplus funds, the discount houses lent to government and local authorities, and bought and sold Treasury Bills, commercial bills, short-dated government securities and short-term local authority bonds.

It had been established practice since the 1930s that the discount houses would tender collectively each week for Treasury Bills and by custom the discount houses were obliged to buy the entire amount issued. If they had insufficient cash in hand to do so, they would seek to borrow from the clearing banks thus reducing the clearing banks' cash. Otherwise they would have to borrow from the Bank at penal rates. The objective of the discount houses was thus to ensure that they had sufficient cash from the clearing banks to cover the weekly tender so that they did not have to borrow from the Bank of England (their lender of last resort) at a punitive rate—the Bank Rate.[115] The Radcliffe report set out the role and special status of the discount houses thus:

> They have a unique place in the functioning of the monetary system in that it is to these houses, and to these alone, that the bank of England operates as lender of last resort. It is, that is to say, through the discount houses that the Bank of England channels the marginal amounts of the cash with which it sees fit to provide the economy: the cash required for the 8 per cent cash reserves of the London clearing banks and the cash required for general circulation.[116]

It was on account of the Bank being the lender of last resort to the discount houses that the clearing banks could lend their surplus cash to the discount houses with complete confidence. The clearing banks thus had at their disposal a means of very short-term, risk-free lending. The discount houses' profits depended upon borrowing (from the clearing banks) at a lower rate than that the rate at which they could lend and the rate at which they could lend was the rate at which they tendered for Treasury Bills. It was struck "by taking a view on the course of Bank Rate during the thirteen weeks' life of the Treasury Bills for which they were about to tender."[117] The Bank was anxious to maintain stability in the Treasury Bill rate in the belief that stability of short-term rates would help preserve stable rates for long-term bonds.[118] Up until 1971 then, the discount market played a stabilizing role in the financial system as a pool of liquidity. It absorbed any short-term cash surpluses from the London clearing banks and utilized these surpluses by buying bills, most notably Treasury Bills. As Kynaston points out, by absorbing surplus cash held by the clearing banks, this market provided "liquidity and lubrication in the financial system" in the period before inter-bank lending and borrowing became common ways of obtaining short-term money.[119]

The activities of the banks were subject to a second form of indirect regulation, that which emanated from the workings of foreign currency exchange controls. First, there were controls over the conversion of sterling into other currencies, a set of controls which had their origins in the Defence (Finance) Regulations issued under the Emergency Powers (Defence) Act 1939, and then through the Exchange Control Act 1947. These controls were progressively relaxed, particularly between 1958 and 1961 at which point the UK and nine other countries agreed to accept their obligations under Article VIII of the Articles of Association of the IMF to maintain the convertibility of their currencies for current transactions. Second, there were controls over the rate of exchange between sterling and other currencies also enshrined in the Articles of Association of the IMF. These prevailed until June 1972 when the pound sterling became a floating currency.

In what respect did exchange controls work as indirect regulatory constraints? First, the Bank delegated day-to-day administration of foreign exchange transactions to banks. The Bank could therefore control which financial institutions could deal in foreign currencies through the authorization process. The banks who were authorized to carry out these transactions under the Exchange Control Act were banks of the highest quality, this authorization being "the highest accolade a bank could attain."[120] Other banks were prohibited from engaging in such transactions. According to Ogus, prior authorization is a high-intensity regulatory intervention. Exchange controls worked as an indirect regulatory constraint in a second way. The system of fixed-but-adjustable exchange rates meant that it was not possible for a large market in speculative foreign currency trading—in which the banks might want to participate—to develop.

2.3 Self-Regulation

Self-regulation by the London clearing banks is this period assumed two forms. First, it took the form of specific regulatory techniques which developed organically from within the clearing banking system itself. The most notable of these were the cash and liquidity ratios which prevailed until 1971, which, as mentioned previously, began as self-regulatory techniques but gravitated to be more in the nature of extra-legal regulation. The second form of self-regulation by the clearing banks was what North described as informal institutions, or "humanly devised constraints," in the form of codes of conduct, customs, sanctions, traditions and taboos. Such institutions, North argues, help create order and reduce uncertainty in exchange.[121] Three brief examples of self-regulation follow. First, there was the agreement between the Big Five since 1918 that they would not amalgamate without government approval. This was described by The *Times* as their "gentleman's agreement."[122] It ended in 1968 with the amalgamation of National Provincial Bank and Westminster Bank. This gentlemen's agreement could be considered as a tradition (it persisted for fifty years) or as a custom. A second example is the adoption by the banks periodically from 1951 to around 1961 of a "self-denying ordinance," an informal agreement between the clearing banks that one bank would not take custom from another by offering better interest rates on deposit accounts or lower commission charges for loans or advances, while government credit restrictions were in force.[123] The ordinance was invoked in May 1951, when the CEOs of the London clearing banks unanimously agreed that a self-denying ordinance should be put in place, initially for a period of six months. The agreement was minuted as follows: "henceforth, for a period of six months, the Banks would not take accounts from one another on the question of terms, whether of interest or of remuneration by way of commission [...]."[124] The "self-denying ordinance" can be thought of as a code of conduct.[125] The third example of self-regulation is a more general one. The London clearing banks had a strong disposition to comply with regulation. Their bias towards compliance was both a component of self-regulation, and underpinned the effectiveness of regulation in its other forms—codified regulation and extra-legal regulation. For example, there is no evidence from the records reviewed that the Bank of England 1946 was not complied with. The fact that as at 1959 the power of direction given to the Bank under the Act had never been used was itself a signal that the banks complied with the authorities' wishes and that therefore the power of direction was not required to be used.[126] Compliance with the cash and liquidity ratios over the period 1946–1966 were shown in Figs. 2.2 and 2.4. Winton reports that in the 1950s Lloyds fell below the liquidity ratio only twice, and from 1963 to 1970 never fell below it at all.[127] In terms of deposit schemes, there is no evidence from the archival records reviewed that the clearing banks did not respond to requests for TDRs or Special Deposits. It is difficult to evaluate with certainty the degree of compliance with quantitative controls. There are a number of references in the minutes of meetings of the CLCB and CEOs to the fact that these controls fell unfairly on the London clearing banks and it could be inferred from this that they at least attempted to comply with these controls. There was one occasion at least in 1969 when a quantitative control was not met. This might suggest that, early on, quantitative controls had an effect on the level of advances made, which implies that there was a high level of compliance with these controls. Later on, they were less effective which might be a sign of lower levels of compliance. Similarly, it is difficult to evaluate with certainty the degree of compliance with qualitative controls although on the other hand, non-compliance does not emerge as a theme within the published and unpublished records reviewed as part of this research. Where particular types of lending were discouraged, it also is difficult to evaluate with certainty the degree of compliance, especially as these discouragements tended to be couched in broad terms (prohibitions on "speculative transactions" or "stockpiling," for example). This would require examining a sample of loan applications to the clearing banks to ascertain the underlying purpose of the loan. There is no evidence from the records reviewed that the self-denying ordinance was not adhered to when invoked. The National Provincial Bank and Westminster Bank broke with the "gentleman's agreement" among the Big Five clearing banks not to amalgamate agreement in 1968.

The purpose of this chapter was to describe the ways in which the London clearing banks were regulated in the quarter-century after the Second World War. The first form of regulation was regulation in its formal and codified guise as law and regulation, beginning with the Bank of England Act 1946. The next form of regulation was less formal and to varying degrees less codified—extra-legal or non-statutory regulation. This form of regulation included quantitative and qualitative guidance to the London clearing banks and controls which influenced the structure of banks' balance sheets. It was a form of regulation underpinned by the Bank of England's power of moral suasion. Third, there was self-regulation, including for example the Big Five's "gentleman's agreement" from 1918 until 1968 that they would not amalgamate. Having considered the nature of clearing bank regulation, the next chapter considers the context within which the clearing banks operated and were regulated, the rationale behind the authorities' approach to regulation, and some of the consequences of the approach.

Notes

1. Barak Orbach, "What Is Regulation?," *Yale Journal on Regulation Online* 30, no. 1 (2012): 6, accessed 20 July 2018, https://papers.ssrn.com/sol3/papers.cfm?abstract_id=2143385##.
2. Philip Selznick, "Focusing Organisational Research on Regulation," in *Regulatory Policy and the Social Sciences*, ed. Roger G. Noll (Berkeley: University of California Press, 1985): 363.
3. Julia Black, "Decentring Regulation: Understanding the Role of Regulation and Self-Regulation in a 'Post-regulatory' World," *Current Legal Problems* 54, no. 1 (2001): 142.
4. Orbach, "What Is Regulation?": 4.
5. "What Is a 'Bank'?" *The Bankers' Almanac and Year Book for 1945–1946*. London: Thomas Skinner & Co (Publishers) Ltd. (page not numbered).
6. Ibid.
7. Ibid.
8. Bank of England Act, 1946, Chapter 27, 4 (1), *legislation.gov.uk*, accessed 13 July 2018, https://www.legislation.gov.uk/ukpga/1946/27/pdfs/ukpga_19460027_en.pdf.
9. Ibid.
10. Committee on the Working of the Monetary System, *Report*, Cmnd. 827, August 1959, para. 350. The Committee had been appointed in May 1957 and was chaired by Lord Radcliffe. It was an ad hoc departmental committee so appointed by a Minister under their conventional powers. According to Davies, "No official report has ever […] shown such scepticism regarding monetary policy in the sense of trying to control the economy by controlling the quantity of money." For a critique of the Radcliffe Report, see Glyn Davies, *A History of Money*, 3rd ed. (Cardiff: University of Wales Press, 2002; reprint, 2010): 401–4.
11. Ibid., para. 350.
12. "The UK Exchange Control: A Short History," *Bank of England Quarterly Bulletin* (Quarter 3, 1967): 246, accessed 12 July 2018, https://www.bankofengland.co.uk/quarterly-bulletin/1967/q3/the-uk-exchange-control-a-short-history.
13. Robb describes how the status of a banking institution was evaluated against a "ladder of recognitions." See Victoria Robb, "The Genesis of Regulation," *Financial Stability Review*, no. 3 (Autumn 1997): 30, accessed 13 July 2018, https://www.bankofengland.co.uk/-/media/boe/files/financial-stability-report/1997/autumn-1997.
14. *Report of the Committee on Company Law Amendment*, Cmd. 6659, June 1945, p. 7. The Committee was chaired by Mr. Justice Cohen.

15. Companies Act 1948, Eighth Schedule, Part III, 23 (3), *legislation.gov.uk*, accessed 13 July 2018, http://www.legislation.gov.uk/ukpga/1948/38/pdfs/ukpga_19480038_en.pdf.
16. Board of Trade, *Report of the Company Law Committee*, Cmnd. 1749, June 1962, para. 399.
17. "Meeting at Board of Trade on 14th April 1966: Definition of a Bank for the Moneylenders Act, 1900," 14 April 1966, TNA IR40/16307: Recognition of banks, s 200 Income Tax Act 1952.
18. Aubrey L. Diamond, "Protection of Depositors Act, 1963," *The Modern Law Review* 26, no. 6 (November 1963): 688–89.
19. *The Licensing and Supervision of Deposit-Taking Institutions*, Cmnd. 6584, August 1976.
20. "The Role of the Banking Supervisor," *Bank of England Quarterly Bulletin* (December 1982): 547, accessed 12 July 2018, https://www.bankofengland.co.uk/quarterly-bulletin/1982/q4/the-role-of-the-banking-supervisor---speech-by-mr-w-p-cooke. The author of the article was the Head of Banking Supervision at the Bank, WP Cooke.
21. "Meeting at Board of Trade on 14th April 1966: Definition of a Bank for the Moneylenders Act, 1900," 14 April 1966, TNA IR40/16307: Recognition of banks, s 200 Income Tax Act 1952.
22. "Supervision of Deposit-Taking Institutions," n.d., TNA T358/214: Working Party on Control and Supervision of the Banking Sector. The other records on the file date from 1975.
23. As a point of contrast, Goddard et al. provide a schedule of legislation impacting on the EU banking and financial sectors between 1977 and 2008. The scale and scope of legislation since 1988 is evident. See John Goddard et al., "European Banking: An Overview," *Journal of Banking & Finance* 31, no. 7 (2007): Table 2, accessed 20 July 2018, https://www.sciencedirect.com/science/article/pii/S0378426607000076?via%3Dihub.
24. Abbott and Snidal suggest that, "The realm of 'soft law' begins once legal arrangements are weakened along one or more of the dimensions of obligation, precision, and delegation." Kenneth W. Abbott and Duncan Snidal, "Hard and Soft Law in International Governance," *International Organisation* 54, no. 3 (Summer 2000): 422.
25. "Bank Liquidity in the United Kingdom," *Bank of England Quarterly Bulletin* (Quarter 4, 1962): 251, accessed 12 July 2018, https://www.bankofengland.co.uk/-/media/boe/files/quarterly-bulletin/1962/bank-liquidity-in-the-united-kingdom.pdf. An exact equivalent of the cash ratio is not applied to UK banks today.
26. "Monthly Statement of Balances of London Clearing Banks," LMA CLC/B/029/MS32193/004-7.

27. "Bank Liquidity in the United Kingdom," *Bank of England Quarterly Bulletin* (Quarter 4, 1962): 249, accessed 12 July 2018, https://www.bankofengland.co.uk/-/media/boe/files/quarterly-bulletin/1962/bank-liquidity-in-the-united-kingdom.pdf.
28. Ibid., 250.
29. Ibid., 250–51.
30. Committee on the Working of the Monetary System, *Report*, Cmnd. 827, August 1959, para. 139.
31. Ibid., para. 352.
32. The NBPI was established in 1965 as a Royal Commission and became a statutory body in 1966.
33. "Bank Liquidity in the United Kingdom," *Bank of England Quarterly Bulletin* (Quarter 4, 1962): 253, accessed 12 July 2018, https://www.bankofengland.co.uk/-/media/boe/files/quarterly-bulletin/1962/bank-liquidity-in-the-united-kingdom.pdf.
34. "Meeting with the Chief Executive Officers, 29 May 1970," 3 June 1970, BoE 8A180/1: Committee of London Clearing Bankers (CLCB) Chief Executive Officers—Minutes of Monthly Meetings.
35. Economic Intelligence Department, Banking Institutions Group, "Clearing Banks' Figures: 15th September 1971," 23 September 1971, BoE 8A180/1: Committee of London Clearing Bankers (CLCB) Chief Executive Officers—Minutes of Monthly Meetings.
36. "Overseas and Foreign Banks in London: 1962–68," *Bank of England Quarterly Bulletin* (Quarter 4, 1968): 160–61, accessed 12 July 2018, https://www.bankofengland.co.uk/quarterly-bulletin/1968/q2/overseas-and-foreign-banks-in-london.
37. Goodhart notes that from early 1971 until March 1971 the new policy was referred to as "A New Approach to Credit Control and the Banking System." From March 1971 the title "Competition and Credit Control" was used. C. A. E. Goodhart, "Competition and Credit Control," Special Paper 229, LSE Financial Markets Group Special Paper Series (March 2014): 1–2.
38. "Competition and Credit Control," *Bank of England Quarterly Bulletin* (Quarter 2, 1971): para. 7, accessed 23 August 2018, https://www.bankofengland.co.uk/-/media/boe/files/quarterly-bulletin/1971/competition-and-credit-control-text-of-a-consultatice-document-issued-on-14-may-1971.
39. Economic Intelligence Department, Banking Institutions Group, "Clearing Banks' Figures: 15th September 1971," 23 September 1971, BoE 8A180/1: Committee of London Clearing Bankers (CLCB) Chief Executive Officers—Minutes of Monthly Meetings.
40. "Today's Meeting with the CEOs," 7 February 1973, BoE 8A180/1: Committee of London Clearing Bankers (CLCB) Chief Executive Officers—Minutes of Monthly Meetings.

41. Henry Clay, *Lord Norman* (London: Macmillan, 1957): 471.
42. "Deposit Rates: The Committee of London Clearing Bankers," 31 July 1940, BoE G15/102: Secretary's Files—Committee of London Clearing Banks (CLCB), British Bankers' Association (BBA), Committee of Scottish Clearing Banks.
43. Statistics Office, 6 March 1944, BoE G15/102: Secretary's Files—Committee of London Clearing Banks (CLCB), British Bankers' Association (BBA), Committee of Scottish Clearing Banks.
44. "Treasury Deposit Receipts," about June 1944, BoE G15/102: Secretary's Files—Committee of London Clearing Banks (CLCB), British Bankers' Association (BBA), Committee of Scottish Clearing Banks.
45. "Official Bank Rate History Data from 1694: Changes in Bank Rate, Minimum Lending Rate, Minimum Band 1 Dealing Rate, Repo Rate and Official Bank Rate, Historical Since 1694," *Bank of England*, accessed 12 July 2018, https://www.bankofengland.co.uk/monetary-policy/the-interest-rate-bank-rate.
46. Pember and Boyle, *British Government Securities in the Twentieth Century: The First Fifty Years, Supplement 1976* (London: Pember and Boyle, 1950): 352.
47. Lloyds Bank Limited Ninetieth Report of Directors and Balance Sheet 31 December 1947, Statement by the Chairman, 1, LBGA HO/S/Rep/8.
48. Report to a Meeting of the Board of Lloyds Bank Limited, "Monthly Statement of Balances of London Clearing Banks May 1947," LBGA HO/D/Boa/Age/17.
49. "Rating Structure Agreed at a Meeting at the Bank of England on 7 November 1951," LMA CLC/B/029/MS32037/007.
50. *Annual Abstract of Statistics No. 92, 1955* (London: HMSO), Table 294.
51. "Monthly Statement of Balances of London Clearing Banks," October 1958, LMA CLC/B/029/MS32193/005 (1954–1959).
52. Margaret Ackrill and Leslie Hannah, *Barclays: The Business of Banking 1690–1996* (Cambridge: Cambridge University Press, 2001): 118.
53. J. R. C. Dow, *The Management of the British Economy, 1945–60* (London: Cambridge University Press, 1970): 241.
54. "Competition and Credit Control," *Bank of England Quarterly Bulletin* (Quarter 2, 1971): para. 6, accessed 23 August 2018, https://www.bankofengland.co.uk/-/media/boe/files/quarterly-bulletin/1971/competition-and-credit-control-text-of-a-consultatice-document-issued-on-14-may-1971.
55. Minutes of a Meeting of the Chief Executive Officers of the Clearing Banks, 30 June 1958, LMA CLC/B/029/MS32037/010.
56. Note on "Credit Control," 22 April 1960, BoE EID4/161 Home Finance: Financial Institutions Other Than Banks—Control of Other Financial Institutions.

57. Minutes of a Meeting of the Chief Executive Officers of the Clearing Banks, 30 June 1958, LMA CLC/B/029/MS32037/010.
58. Ibid.
59. Ibid.
60. Chancellor [Derick Heathcoat Amory] to the Governor, 1 July 1958, LMA CLC/B/029/MS32259/004.
61. Chancellor to the Chairman of the Capital Issues Committee, 1 July 1958, LMA CLC/B/029/MS32037/010.
62. C. F. Cobbold, speech at a dinner given by the Lord Mayor to the Bankers and Merchants of the City of London, 16 October 1958, LSE Piercy Collection 9/73: Banks.
63. Ibid.
64. Governor to the Chancellor of the Exchequer, 3 July 1958, LMA CLC/B/029/MS32259/004.
65. "Extracts from Recent Speeches by the Governor of the Bank of England," given at the Lord Mayor's dinner to the bankers and merchants of the City of London on 17 October 1968, *Bank of England Quarterly Bulletin* (Quarter 4, 1968): 411, accessed 12 July 2018, https://www.bankofengland.co.uk/quarterly-bulletin/1968/q4/extracts-from-recent-speeches-by-the-governor-of-the-bank-of-england.
66. On 20 August 1981 a new Special Deposits Scheme was announced which would apply to all institutions with eligible liabilities of £10 million or more. "Monetary Control—Provisions," *Bank of England Quarterly Bulletin* (Quarter 3, 1981): 348, accessed 12 July 2018, https://www.bankofengland.co.uk/quarterly-bulletin/1981/q3/monetary-control-provisions---paper-issued-by-the-bank-on-5-august.
67. Goodhart, "Competition and Credit Control," 13.
68. Bank of England, "The Control of Bank Lending," 19 May 1967, TNA T326/652: Financial Control of Overseas Banks and Accepting Houses in the United Kingdom.
69. "Control of Lending of Outside Banks," 7 June 1967, TNA T326/652: Financial Control of Overseas Banks and Accepting Houses in the United Kingdom. The Radcliffe Committee had identified seventy-five "overseas and foreign banks" and by 1978 there were 201 overseas banks; see Committee to Review the Functioning of Financial Institutions, *Report*, Cmnd. 7937, June 1980, Appendix 3, 3.4.
70. "Cash Deposits," 12 December 1967, TNA T326/793: Financial Control of Overseas Banks and Accepting Houses in the United Kingdom.
71. Ackrill and Hannah, *Barclays: The Business of Banking 1690–1996*, 160.
72. "Deposit Rates: The Committee of London Clearing Bankers," 31 July 1940, BoE G15/102: Secretary's Files—Committee of London Clearing Banks (CLCB), British Bankers' Association (BBA), Committee of Scottish Clearing Banks.

73. Fforde was Chief Cashier at the Bank from 1966 to 1970 and Executive Director (Home Finance) from 1970 to 1982.
74. Charles A. E. Goodhart, "Competition and Credit Control: Some Personal Reflections," *Financial History Review* 22, no. 2 (2015): Appendix A. Fforde's note was dated 24 December 1970 and marked 'Top Secret'.
75. David Kynaston, *The City of London. Volume IV: A Club No More, 1945–2000* (London: Pimlico, 2002): 437.
76. Forrest Capie, *The Bank of England: 1950s to 1979* (Cambridge: Cambridge University Press, 2010): 483–523.
77. Kynaston, *The City of London. Volume IV: A Club No More, 1945–2000*, 102–3.
78. C. F. Cobbold, speech at a dinner given by the Lord Mayor to the Bankers and Merchants of the City of London, 16 October 1958, LSE Piercy Collection 9/73: Banks.
79. Treasury Chambers, "The Clearing Banks' Cartel: Report of the Banking Study Group," 12 May 1969, BoE C40/1325: Banking and Banking Practice Interest Rates and Charges.
80. To encourage exports, as a way of managing the risks, exports could be guaranteed by the Export Credits Guarantee Department. At the time of Radcliffe report, about 16% of all UK exports were insured by the Export Credits Guarantee Department against political, exchange, and commercial risk. Committee on the Working of the Monetary System, *Report*, Cmnd. 827, August 1959, para. 874.
81. Informal Note of Special Meeting of the Committee of London Clearing Bankers, 21 November 1968, LMA CLC/B/029/MS 32259/006.
82. Memorandum by D.C.G.M. to a Meeting of the Board of Lloyds Bank Limited, "Export and Shipbuilding Finance," 30 March 1973, LBGA HO/D/Boa/Age/43.
83. Memorandum to a Meeting of the Board of Lloyds Bank Limited, "Export and Shipbuilding Finance," 31 March 1978, LBGA HO/D/Boa/Age/48.
84. Memorandum to a Meeting of the Board of Lloyds Bank Limited, "Export and Shipbuilding Finance," 29 March 1974, LBGA HO/D/Boa/Age/44.
85. The Committee of London Clearing Bankers, *The London Clearing Banks: Evidence by the Committee of London Clearing Bankers to the Committee to Review the Functioning of Financial Institutions, November 1977* (London: Longman Group Limited, 1978): Table 58.
86. Committee to Review the Functioning of Financial Institutions, *Report*, Cmnd. 7937, June 1980, Appendix 3, para. 3.249.

87. "Announcement to the Public Respecting Proposals for the Creation of a Company Owned Collectively by the Banks," 1944, LSE Piercy Collection 9/83: Committee of London Clearing Bankers.
88. Richard Coopey, "The First Venture Capitalist: Financing Development in Britain after 1945, the Case of ICFC/3i," *Business and Economic History* 23, no. 1 (1994): 264.
89. "Aide Memoire for the Press to Accompany the Announcement to the Public," 1944, LSE Piercy Collection 9/83: Committee of London Clearing Bankers.
90. Note by Lord Piercy, "Clearing Bankers and ICFC," 12 September 1955, LSE Piercy Collection 9/83: Committee of London Clearing Bankers. William Piercy chaired the Industrial and Commercial Finance Corporation Limited from its inception until 1964. After a career in business and the City, Piercy became a special assistant in the Export Credit Guarantee Department in 1940 and 1941 and later served as principal assistant to the deputy prime minister, Clement Attlee. During the war he became a member of the Labour Party. He was a director of the Bank of England from 1946 to 1956. See *Oxford Dictionary of National Biography*, Oxford University Press, 2004, s.v. "Piercy, William Stuckey, first Baron Piercy (1886–1966)," Martin Chick, accessed 7 March 2016, http://www.oxforddnb.com/view/article/35528; and *Who Was Who*, A & C Black, an imprint of Bloomsbury Publishing plc, 1920–2016; online ed., Oxford University Press, 2014; online ed., April 2014, s.v. "Piercy, 1st Baron," accessed 7 March 2016, http://www.ukwhoswho.com/view/article/oupww/whowaswho/U47531.
91. Clay, *Lord Norman*, 470. The CIC became less active after 1959 and in November 1967 was formally dissolved.
92. *Capital Issues Control: Memorandum of Guidance to the Capital Issues Committee*, Cmd. 6645, May 1945, para. 1.
93. Ibid., para. 7
94. *Capital Issues Control: Special Memorandum to the Capital Issues Committee*, Cmd. 7281, December 1947.
95. Ibid.
96. See Kenneth Gooding, "End of the Capital Issues Committee," *Financial Times*, 11 November 1967, Financial Times Historical Archive 1888–2010, Gale Cengage Learning.
97. Chancellor [Sir John Anderson] of the Exchequer to the Governor, 24 May 1945, LMA CLC/B/029/MS32259/001. An inherent difficulty was how to define speculation and how to distinguish it from normal business transaction, such as when a producer bought raw material in advance if they anticipated that prices would rise.
98. Chancellor of the Exchequer [Sir Stafford Cripps] to the Governor, 2 December 1947, LMA CLC/B/029/MS32259/001.

99. Chancellor of the Exchequer [Derick Heathcoat Amory] to the Chair of the Capital Issues Committee [Lord Kennet], 1 July 1958, LMA CLC/B/029/MS32259/004.
100. "Bank of England," 24 July 1961 LMA CLC/B/029/MS32259/005.
101. "Britain's Clearing Bankers regain freedom to lend," *Times*, 29 October 1962, The Times Digital Archive 1785–2010, Gale Cengage Learning.
102. Anthony Ogus, *Regulation: Legal Form and Economic Theory* (Oxford: Hart Publishing, 2004): 4–5.
103. J. R. Winton, *Lloyds Bank, 1918–1969* (Oxford: Oxford University Press, 1982): 80.
104. Note, 15 March 1960, T233/2082 Monthly Exchequer and Monetary Figures including Clearing Banks' Monthly Statement Analysis.
105. Committee on the Working of the Monetary System, *Report*, Cmnd. 827, August 1959, para. 813.
106. As an example, see Committee of London Clearing Bankers' Statistical Unit, "Balances of the London Clearing Banks as at 18th February 1976," TNA T386/183: Banks' Reserve Ratio and Eligible Liabilities and the Monthly Statement of the London Clearing Banks.
107. John Turner, *Banking in Crisis: The Rise and Fall of British Banking Stability, 1800 to the Present* (Cambridge: Cambridge University Press, 2014): 185.
108. Bernard Attard, "Moral Suasion, Empire Borrowers and the New Issue Market During the 1920s," in *The British Government and the City of London in the Twentieth Century*, ed. Ranald Michie and Philip Williamson (Cambridge: Cambridge University Press, 2004): 200.
109. Andreas Busch, "National Filters: Europeanisation, Institutions, and Discourse in the Case of Banking Regulation," *West European Politics* 27, no. 2 (2004): 314. Busch contrasts the system of bank supervision which prevailed for a century up to the 1970s characterized by "flexibility and informality" with the period of more formal supervision from the 1970s to 1997. Ibid., 314–18.
110. "Supervision of Deposit-Taking Institutions," n.d., TNA T358/214: Working Party on Control and Supervision of the Banking Sector. The other records on the file date from 1975.
111. "The Old Lady of Threadneedle Street," *The Money Programme*, ed. John Dekker, featuring Sir Alex Cairncross, Lord Cromer, Sir Eric Faulkner and Sir Jasper Hollom, aired 26 November 1976 on the BBC, British Film Institute Reuben Library: 610012.
112. Heidi Mandanis Schooner and Michael Taylor, "Convergence and Competition: The Case of Bank Regulation in Britain and the United States," *Michigan Journal of International Law* 20, no. 4 (Summer 1999): 621.

113. Kenneth E. Boulding, "The Legitimacy of Central Banks," (Steering Committee for the Fundamental Reappraisal of the Discount Mechanism Appointed by the Board of Governors of the Federal Reserve System, 1969): 1, accessed 23 August 2018, https://fraser.stlouisfed.org/docs/historical/federal%20reserve%20history/discount-mech/legcent_boulding.pdf.
114. R. S. Sayers, *Central Banking After Bagehot* (Oxford: The Clarendon Press, 1957): 45–46.
115. The Bank Rate would normally be between 1 and 1.75% above the rate at which they could borrow from the clearing banks or other banks. Technically, the Bank Rate was "the rate of interest payable on loans or rediscounts by the Discount Office [...] which may be more strictly defined as the minimum rate at which the Bank of England stands ready to lend at last resort to a discount house." See Committee on the Working of the Monetary System, *Report*, Cmnd. 827, August 1959, para. 358.
116. Committee on the Working of the Monetary System, *Report*, Cmnd. 827, August 1959, para. 162.
117. Ibid., para. 170.
118. Ibid., para. 583.
119. Kynaston, *The City of London. Volume IV: A Club No More, 1945–2000*, 55.
120. Robb, "The Genesis of Regulation": 30. Robb sets out five pre-1979 statuses on the ladder of recognitions under the various statues.
121. Douglass C. North, "Institutions," *Journal of Economic Perspectives* 5, no. 1 (Winter 1991): 97.
122. "Place of Mergers in British Banking: Control by Gentlemen's Agreement," *Times*, 15 August 1962, The Times Digital Archive 1785–2010, Gale Cengage Learning.
123. *Oxford English Dictionary*, OED Online, s.v. "self-deˈny-ing, adj.," accessed 23 August 2018, http://www.oed.com/view/Entry/175198?redirectedFrom=self-denying+ordinance#eid1217307290. In extended use, the self-denying ordinance denotes "any rule, law, regulation, etc., by which a person deprives himself or herself of some advantage or benefit."
124. Minutes of a Meeting of the Chief Executive Officers of Clearing Banks, 10 May 1951, LMA CLC/B/029/MS32037/007.
125. See Linda Arch, "Disposed Towards Self-Restraint: The London Clearing Banks, 1946–71," in *The Challenges of Capitalism for Virtue Ethics and the Common Good: Interdisciplinary Perspectives*, ed. Kleio Akrivou and Alejo José G. Sison (Cheltenham: Edward Elgar Publishing Limited, 2016): 78–79.
126. Committee on the Working of the Monetary System, *Report*, Cmnd. 827, August 1959, para. 350.
127. Winton, *Lloyds Bank, 1918–1969*, 164.

References

Primary Sources: Unpublished

Bank of England Archive

6A127/1: Economic Intelligence Department: Hire Purchase
8A180/1: Committee of London Clearing Bankers (CLCB) Chief Executive Officers—Minutes of Monthly Meetings
C40/1325: Cashier's Department: Chief Cashier's Policy Files: Banking and Banking Practice: Interest Rates and Charges
EID4/161: Economic Intelligence Department: Records of Home Finance: Financial Institutions Other Than Banks—Control of Other Financial Institutions
G15/102: Secretary's Files: Committee of London Clearing Banks (CLCB), British Bankers' Association (BBA), Committee of Scottish Clearing Banks

Lloyds Banking Group Archive

HO/D/Boa/Age/17
HO/D/Boa/Age/41–44
HO/D/Boa/Age/46–48
HO/S/Rep/8–19

London Metropolitan Archives

MS32037: Committee of London Clearing Bankers and Chief Executive Officers' Committee Minutes (2/7a and 2/7/1)
MS32193: Statistics C/B Monthly Statements of Weekly Balances of Clearing Banks
MS32259: Credit Restriction—Banks and HM Government
MS34844: General Correspondence, Mainly with Banks

London School of Economics and Political Science Library, Archives and Special Collections

Piercy 9 (9/73, 9/80, 9/83)

The National Archives

IR40/16307: Recognition of Banks, s. 200 Income Tax Act 1952
T233/2082: Monthly Exchequer and Monetary Figures including Clearing Banks' Monthly Statement Analysis
T326/652: Financial Control of Overseas Banks and Accepting Houses in the UK, 1964–1967
T326/793: Financial Control of Overseas Banks and Accepting Houses in the UK, 1967–1968

T358/214: Working Party on Control and Supervision of the Banking Sector

T386/183: Banks' Reserve Ratio and Eligible Liabilities and the Monthly Statement of the London Clearing Banks

Primary Sources: Published

Books and Pamphlets

The Bankers' Almanac and Year Book for 1945–1946. London: Thomas Skinner & Co (Publishers) Ltd., 1945–1946.

Competition and Credit Control. Bank of England, May 1971.

Command Papers

Capital Issues Control: Memorandum of Guidance to the Capital Issues Committee, Cmd. 6645, May 1945.

Board of Trade, *Report of the Committee on Company Law Amendment*, Cmd. 6659, June 1945.

Capital Issues Control: Special Memorandum to the Capital Issues Committee, Cmd. 7281, December 1947.

Committee on the Working of the Monetary System, *Report*, Cmnd. 827, August 1959.

Board of Trade, *Report of the Company Law Committee*, Cmnd. 1749, June 1962.

The Licensing and Supervision of Deposit-Taking Institutions, Cmnd. 6584, August 1976.

Committee to Review the Functioning of Financial Institutions, *Report*, Cmnd. 7937, June 1980.

Newspapers and Magazines

Financial Times

Times

Television Programmes

British Film Institute Reuben Library: Film and Television Works Collection

Secondary Sources

Books and Articles

Abbott, Kenneth W., and Duncan Snidal. "Hard and Soft Law in International Governance." *International Organisation* 54, no. 3 (Summer 2000): 421–56.

Ackrill, Margaret, and Leslie Hannah. *Barclays: The Business of Banking 1690–1996*. Cambridge: Cambridge University Press, 2001.
Arch, Linda. "Disposed Towards Self-Restraint: The London Clearing Banks, 1946–71." In *The Challenges of Capitalism for Virtue Ethics and the Common Good: Interdisciplinary Perspectives*, edited by Kleio Akrivou and Alejo José G. Sison, 75–89. Cheltenham: Edward Elgar Publishing Limited, 2016.
Attard, Bernard. "Moral Suasion, Empire Borrowers and the New Issue Market During the 1920s." In *The British Government and the City of London in the Twentieth Century*, edited by Ranald Michie and Philip Williamson. Cambridge: Cambridge University Press, 2004.
Black, Julia. "Decentring Regulation: Understanding the Role of Regulation and Self-Regulation in a 'Post-regulatory' World." *Current Legal Problems* 54, no. 1 (2001): 103–46.
Boulding, Kenneth E. *The Legitimacy of Central Banks*: Steering Committee for the Fundamental Reappraisal of the Discount Mechanism Appointed by the Board of Governors of the Federal Reserve System, 1969. Accessed 23 August 2018. https://fraser.stlouisfed.org/docs/historical/federal%20reserve%20history/discountmech/legcent_boulding.pdf.
Busch, Andreas. "National Filters: Europeanisation, Institutions, and Discourse in the Case of Banking Regulation." *West European Politics* 27, no. 2 (2004): 310–33.
Capie, Forrest. *The Bank of England: 1950s to 1979*. Cambridge: Cambridge University Press, 2010.
Clay, Henry. *Lord Norman*. London: Macmillan, 1957.
The Committee of London Clearing Bankers. *The London Clearing Banks: Evidence by the Committee of London Clearing Bankers to the Committee to Review the Functioning of Financial Institutions, November 1977*. London: Longman Group Limited, 1978.
Coopey, Richard. "The First Venture Capitalist: Financing Development in Britain After 1945, the Case of ICFC/3i." *Business and Economic History* 23, no. 1 (1994): 262–71.
Davies, Glyn. *A History of Money*. 3rd ed. Cardiff: University of Wales Press, 2002. Reprint, 2010.
Diamond, Aubrey L. "Protection of Depositors Act, 1963." *The Modern Law Review* 26, no. 6 (November 1963): 680–90.
Dow, J. R. C. *The Management of the British Economy, 1945–60*. London: Cambridge University Press, 1970.
Goddard, John, Philip Molyneux, John O. S. Wilson, and Manouche Tavakoli. "European Banking: An Overview." *Journal of Banking & Finance* 31, no. 7 (2007). Accessed 20 July 2018. https://www.sciencedirect.com/science/article/pii/S0378426607000076?via%3Dihub: 1911–35.

Goodhart, C. A. E. "Competition and Credit Control." Special Paper 229, LSE Financial Markets Group Special Paper Series (March 2014).

Goodhart, C. A. E. "Competition and Credit Control: Some Personal Reflections." *Financial History Review* 22, no. 2 (2015): 235–46.

Kynaston, David. *The City of London. Volume IV: A Club No More, 1945–2000.* London: Pimlico, 2002.

North, Douglass C. "Institutions." *Journal of Economic Perspectives* 5, no. 1 (Winter 1991): 97–112.

Ogus, Anthony. *Regulation: Legal Form and Economic Theory.* Oxford: Hart Publishing, 2004.

Orbach, Barak. "What Is Regulation?" *Yale Journal on Regulation Online* 30, no. 1 (2012). Accessed 20 July 2018. https://papers.ssrn.com/sol3/papers.cfm?abstract_id=2143385##.

Pember and Boyle. *British Government Securities in the Twentieth Century: The First Fifty Years, Supplement 1976.* London: Pember and Boyle, 1950.

Robb, Victoria. "The Genesis of Regulation." *Financial Stability Review*, no. 3 (Autumn 1997). Accessed 13 July 2018. https://www.bankofengland.co.uk/-/media/boe/files/financial-stability-report/1997/autumn-1997.

Sayers, R. S. *Central Banking After Bagehot.* Oxford: The Clarendon Press, 1957.

Schooner, Heidi Mandanis, and Michael Taylor. "Convergence and Competition: The Case of Bank Regulation in Britain and the United States." *Michigan Journal of International Law* 20, no. 4 (Summer 1999): 595–656.

Selznick, Philip. "Focusing Organisational Research on Regulation." In *Regulatory Policy and the Social Sciences*, edited by Roger G. Noll, 363–67. Berkeley: University of California Press, 1985.

Turner, John. *Banking in Crisis: The Rise and Fall of British Banking Stability, 1800 to the Present.* Cambridge: Cambridge University Press, 2014.

Winton, J. R. *Lloyds Bank, 1918–1969.* Oxford: Oxford University Press, 1982.

CHAPTER 3

Context, Rationale and Consequences

Abstract This chapter provides an overview of the economic and industry context within which the London clearing banks operated. It argues that the need to maintain the stability and value of the pound sterling was a key factor in understanding the approach to regulation adopted, rather than the need to minimize the cost of government debt by the policy of financial repression. The chapter evaluates the argument that the nature of bank regulation led to parts of the financial and banking system (such as the euromarkets and the secondary—or fringe—banks) being too lightly, or even unregulated, and that this regulatory neglect contributed to the secondary banking crisis which broke in December 1973. Finally, it explores the regulatory, institutional and structural factors which stabilized banking by acting as counterweights to excessive risk-taking by the clearing banks.

Keywords Financial repression · Balance of payments on current account · Secondary banking crisis · Competition and Credit Control · Risk in banking

3.1 Post-war Regulation in Context

Bank regulation in the period from 1946 until the 1970s was concerned not only with ensuring the stability of the banking system but also with advancing monetary policy objectives. Bank regulatory policy

© The Author(s) 2018

L. Arch, *The Regulation of the London Clearing Banks, 1946–1971*, Palgrave Studies in Economic History,
https://doi.org/10.1007/978-3-030-00910-6_3

and monetary policy were tightly integrated. This interrelationship has been explored by Allen for the period 1951–1959, and by Tew and Artis for the period 1960–1974.[1] Aikman, Bush and Taylor have compared the impact of monetary policy instruments with the impact of macro-prudential instruments in the period of the Radcliffe report.[2] In 1959, that report had summarized the objectives of monetary policy thus:

1. A high and stable level of employment;
2. Reasonable stability of the internal purchasing power of money;
3. Steady economic growth and improvement of the standard of living;
4. Some contribution, implying a margin in the balance of payments, to the economic development of the outside world;
5. A strengthening of London's international reserves, implying further margin in the balance of payments.[3]

The fact that at times it was difficult to see where regulatory policy ended and monetary policy began lends particular significance to the economic context within which bank regulation occurred. Figures 3.1, 3.2, 3.3, 3.4, 3.5, 3.6, 3.7, 3.8, 3.9, and 3.10 illustrate the some of the key economic and market trends in the period 1946 to the late 1970s and are followed by a comment on their significance for bank regulation.[4]

One broad observation to be made is that in a number of respects, the economic position of the UK was deteriorating into the 1970s. This can be seen, for example, with respect to unemployment (which until mid-1971 was almost continuously below 4% but higher thereafter), the balance of payments on current account, and particularly with respect to inflation as reflected in the Retail Price Index.[5] While the Retail Price Index increased very significantly over the entire period—from 51 in 1946 to 414 in 1979—increases were particularly marked in the 1970s. Key macroeconomic variables were also tending to become more volatile in the late 1960s and 1970s. This was the case with the exchange rate between the US dollar and the pound sterling after the disintegration of the fixed-but-adjustable exchange rate system in 1971–1973. The index of real gross domestic product per head was more volatile in the 1970s, even decreasing in 1974 (from 130 to 129) and 1975 (from 129 to 127). The house price index showed rapid rises in house prices in both the early 1970s and late 1970s. The share price index increased significantly over the period and was volatile from the late nineteen-sixties.

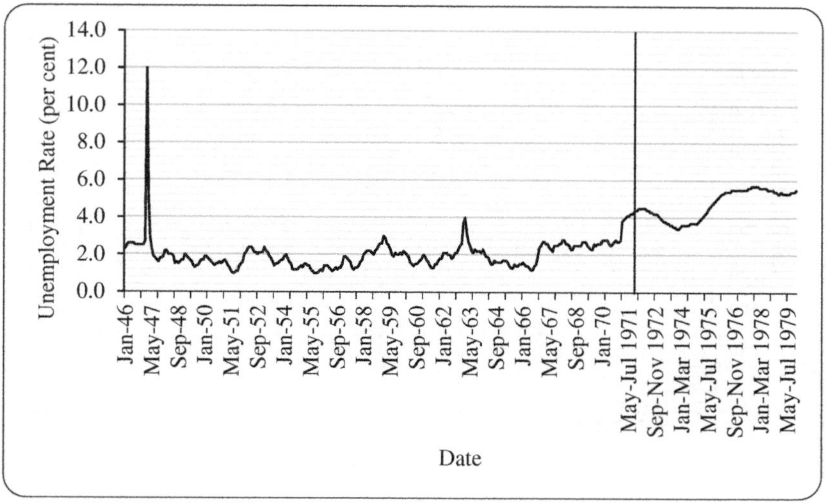

Fig. 3.1 Unemployment rate, January 1946 to October–December 1979 (*Sources* (i) For the period from January, 1946: James Denman and Paul McDonald, "Unemployment Statistics from 1881 to the Present Day," *Labour Market Trends* 104, no. 1 (January 1996): 7, Labour Market Statistics Group, Central Statistical Office; (ii) For the period from quarter 1, 1971: "Time Series: Unemployment Rate (Aged 16 and Over, Seasonally Adjusted)," *Office for National Statistics*, accessed 13 July 2018, https://www.ons.gov.uk/employmentandlabourmarket/peoplenotinwork/unemployment#timeseries. *Note* The new policy, Competition and Credit Control, was introduced in September 1971 as indicated by the vertical line)

The general trend in the Bank Rate was for it to increase, but the period was also marked by two long periods of negative real interest rates. On the other hand, government debt as a percentage of gross domestic product decreased almost continuously throughout the period. Although it fluctuated, there was a strong overall growth trend in the household savings ratio. By the 1970s then, the economic landscape was marked by volatility with respect to key economic and market indicators and by very high general price inflation.

The period of greater fragility in banking from the early 1970s onwards occurred against a backdrop of change in the international economic order. On 15 August 1971, US president Richard Nixon closed

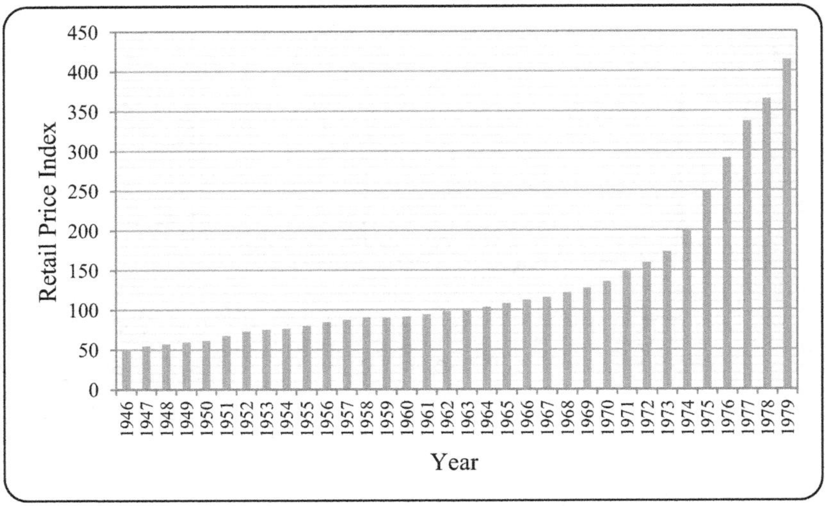

Fig. 3.2 Retail Price Index, 1946–1979 (*Source* David Butler and Gareth Butler, *Twentieth-Century British Political Facts 1900–2000*, 8th ed. [Basingstoke: Palgrave Macmillan, 2000. Reprint, 2005]: 411. *Note* 1963 = 100)

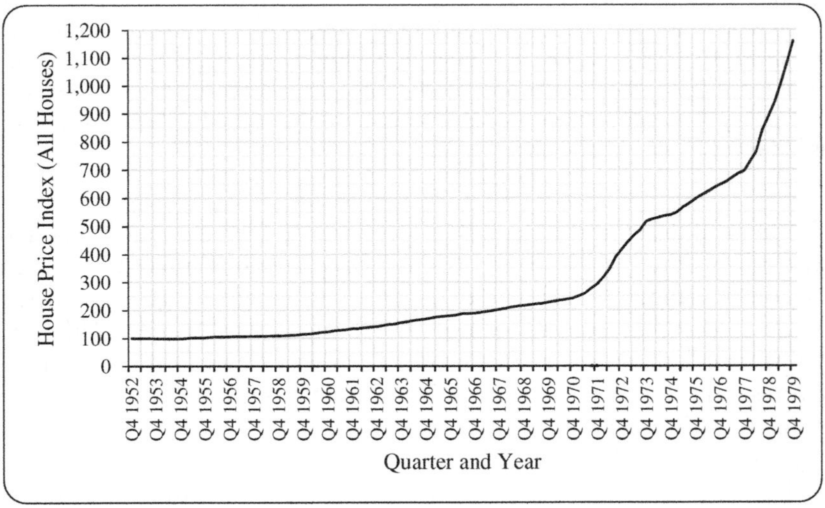

Fig. 3.3 UK house price index (all houses): quarter 4, 1952–quarter 4, 1979 (*Source* "UK House Prices Since 1952," *Nationwide Building Society*, accessed 5 July 2017, http://www.nationwide.co.uk/~/media/MainSite/documents/about/house-price-index/downloads/uk-house-price-since-1952.xls. *Note* Q4 1952 = 100)

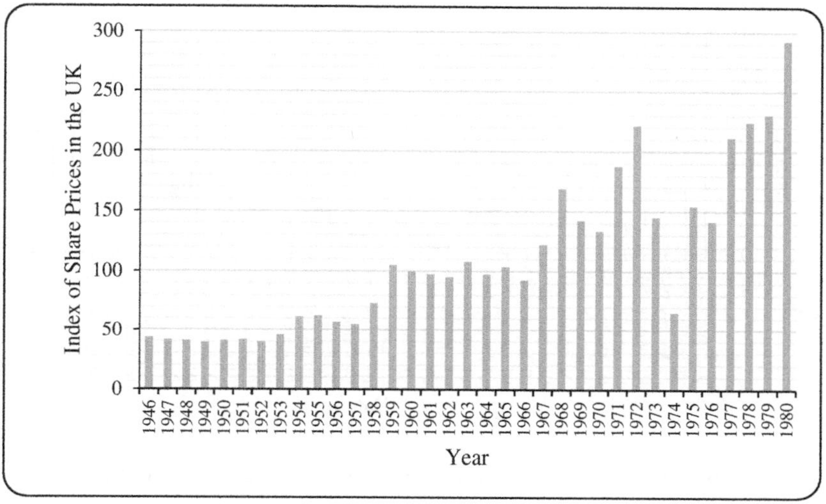

Fig. 3.4 Index of annual share prices in the UK, 1 January 1946–1 January 1980 (*Source* "Share Prices in the United Kingdom [SPPUKA]," Bank of England, retrieved from *FRED Economic Data St. Louis Fed*, accessed 24 July 2018, https://fred.stlouisfed.org/series/SPPUKA. *Note* April 1962 = 100)

the "gold window" when he announced that foreign central banks would no longer be able to convert their US dollars into gold, one component of his New Economic Policy, known as the "Nixon shock."[6] The ending of the convertibility of US dollars into gold precipitated the demise of the fixed-but-adjustable exchange rate system established under the Articles of Agreement of the International Monetary Fund (IMF). Nixon's action was the culmination of a series of changes in currency exchange rates that had occurred over the preceding four years: a devaluation of the pound sterling in November 1967, a devaluation of the French franc in August 1969, a revaluation of the German mark in October 1969 and the mark becoming a floating currency from May 1971. A press release from Conservative Central Office on 9 September 1971 captured precisely how far-reaching these changes were:

> Since the war we had a system of stable exchange rates and, although that system has been under strain in recent years, on the whole it has worked pretty well. Now it has broken down. […] The problems which have arisen in the past few weeks are immense and complex, and it is an illusion to

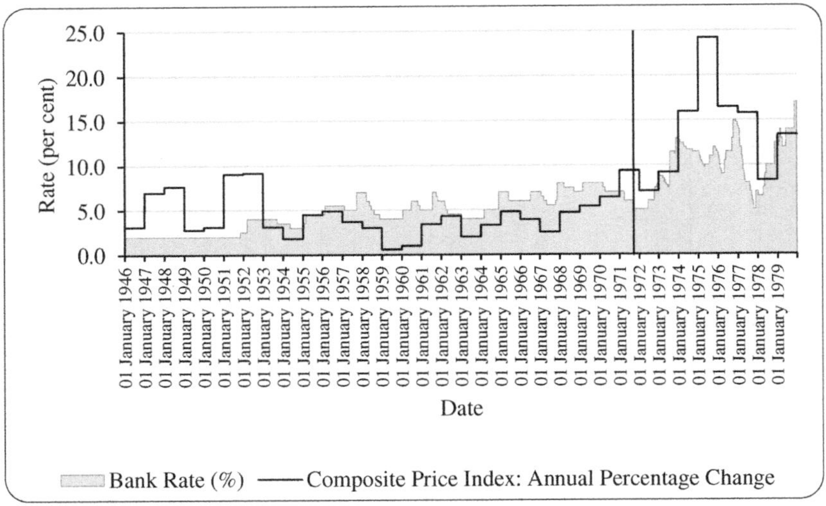

Fig. 3.5 Daily bank rate and annual inflation rates, 1946–1979 (*Sources* (i) "RPI All Items: Percentage change Over 12 Months: Jan 1987 = 100," *Office for National Statistics*, accessed 30 April 2017, https://www.ons.gov.uk/economy/inflationandpriceindices/timeseries/czbh/mm23; (ii) Jim O'Donoghue, Louise Goulding and Grahame Allen, "Consumer Price Inflation Since 1750," *Economic Trends 604*, March 2004, 44, Table 2, accessed 14 April 2017, http://webarchive.nationalarchives.gov.uk/20160105160709/ http://ons.gov.uk/ons/rel/elmr/economic-trends--discontinued-/no--604--march-2004/index.html; (iii) "Official Bank Rate History Data from 1694: Changes in Bank Rate, Minimum Lending Rate, Minimum Band 1 Dealing Rate, Repo Rate and Official Bank Rate, Historical Since 1694," *Bank of England*, accessed 12 July 2018, https://www.bankofengland.co.uk/monetary-policy/the-interest-rate-bank-rate. From 16 October 1972, the rate shown is the Minimum Lending Rate. The bank rates shown are daily rates. *Note* The new policy, Competition and Credit Control, was introduced in September 1971 as indicated by the vertical line)

> think that they can be solved quickly. Our task must be to find a realistic pattern of rates to keep trade going on a reasonable basis. But that is not enough. We also have to work out a new basis for the international system, and that will inevitably take longer.[7]

On 17 and 18 December 1971, representatives of the G10 countries met at the Smithsonian Institution in Washington DC, where new exchange rates were agreed, and the US dollar was devalued in relation to gold from $35 per ounce to $38 per ounce. Wider exchange rate bands within

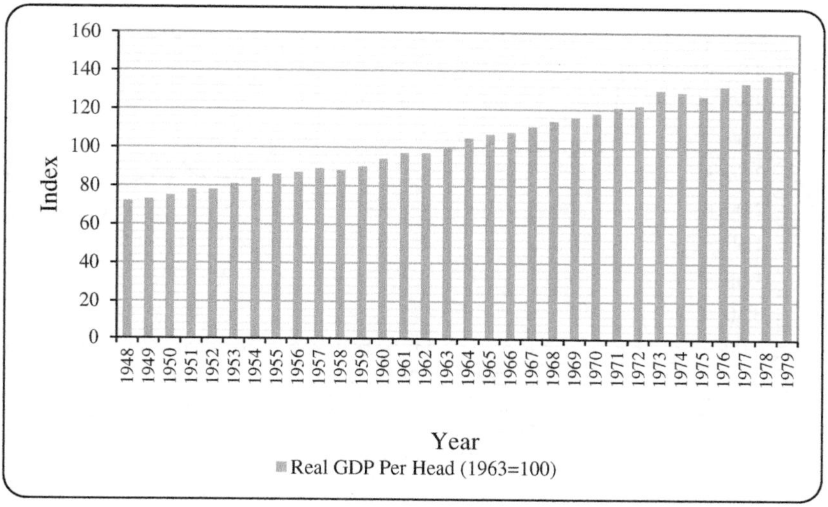

Fig. 3.6 Index of real GDP per head, 1948–1979 (*Source* David Butler and Gareth Butler, *Twentieth-Century British Political Facts 1900–2000*, 8th ed. [Basingstoke: Palgrave Macmillan, 2000. Reprint, 2005]: 411)

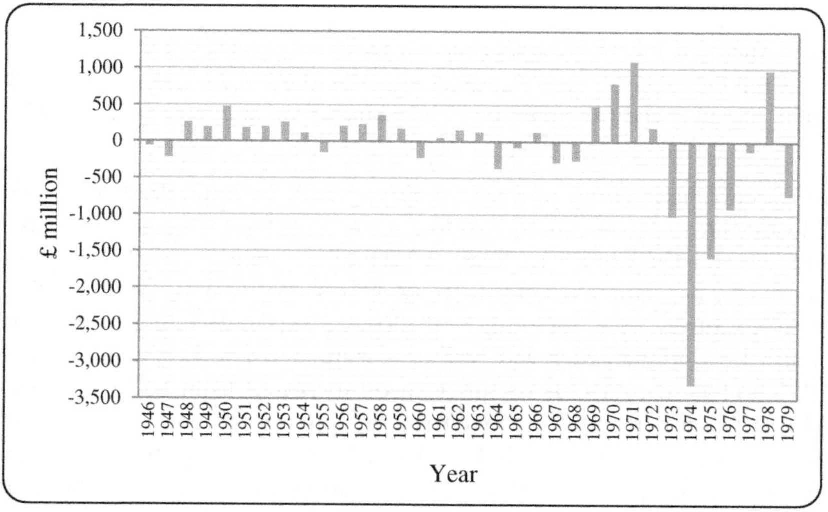

Fig. 3.7 Nominal overall current balance (£ million), 1946–1979 (*Source* B. R. Mitchell, *British Historical Statistics* [Cambridge: Cambridge University Press, 2011], National Accounts 15. B. 1870–1980, pp. 872–73)

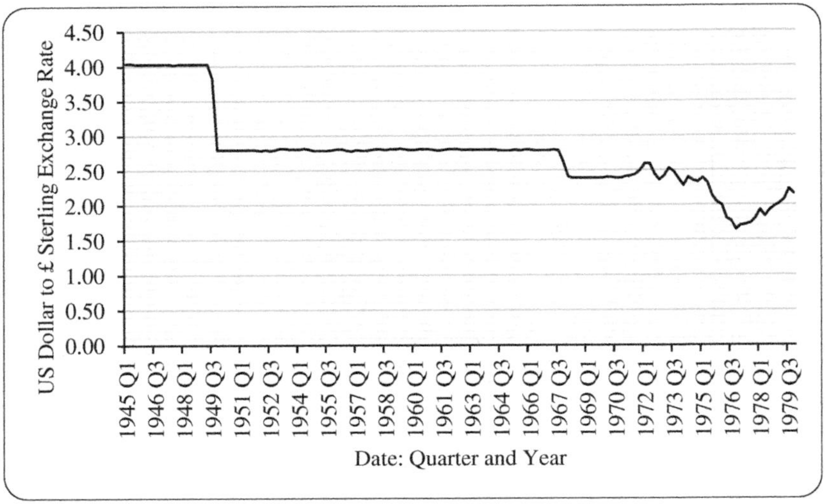

Fig. 3.8 Quarterly sterling-US dollar exchange rate, 1945–1979 (*Source* "Bank of England, US/UK Foreign Exchange Rate in the United Kingdom (USUKFXUKQ)," *FRED, Federal Reserve Bank of St. Louis*, accessed 24 July 2018, https://fred.stlouisfed.org/series/USUKFXUKQ. The underlying sources of the data are: Lawrence H. Officer, *Between the Dollar-Sterling Gold Points: Exchange Rates, Parity, and Market Behavior* [Cambridge: Cambridge University Press, 1996], *Federal Reserve Banking and Monetary Statistics 1914–41* and *1941–1970*, and Office for National Statistics [series ID: AUSS]. *Note* Sterling was devalued in July 1949 and November 1967. It became a floating currency in June 1972)

which currencies could move were also agreed. In June 1972, however, Edward Heath's government broke from the Smithsonian agreement and allowed the pound to float. A second devaluation of the US dollar to \$42 per ounce occurred on 12 February 1973. By March 1973, many countries were operating with floating exchange rates.[8] The international economic order was further disrupted when, between October 1973 and January 1974, the price of oil increased from \$2.90 per barrel to \$11.65 per barrel following the oil embargo on the United States by the Organisation of Arab Petroleum Exporting Countries. Thus by late 1973, the pound sterling was a floating currency, the system of fixed-but-adjustable exchange rates had dissolved, and the world was in the midst of an oil price crisis.

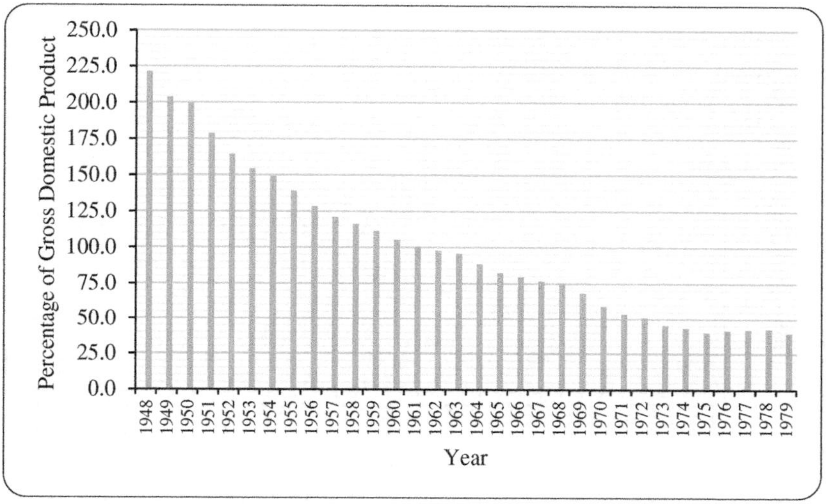

Fig. 3.9 Government debt as a percentage of gross domestic product, 1948–1979 (*Sources* (i) GDP at Current Prices (YBHA): "United Kingdom Economic Accounts: Main Aggregates," *Office for National Statistics*, accessed 24 July 2018, https://www.ons.gov.uk/economy/nationalaccounts/uksectoraccounts/datasets/unitedkingdomeconomicaccountsmainaggregates; (ii) National Debt: 1948–78: *Annual Abstract of Statistics 1952*, Table 258, *1960*, Table 292, *1969*, Table 324, *1979*, Table 16.16; 1979: David Butler and Gareth Butler, *Twentieth Century British Political Facts 1900–2000*, 8th ed. [Basingstoke: Palgrave Macmillan, 2005]: 424)

The volatility in the domestic economy intensified in 1972 and 1973. Prices increased during 1973 by 9.2% and were to increase by 16% and 24.2%, respectively over the next two years.[9] The money stock (measured by sterling M3) was £20,111 million at the end of 1971, shortly after the introduction of CCC, but £32,046 million at the end of 1973, an increase of 59% over that two-year period, CCC having abolished many of the controls on bank lending.[10] The philosophy of CCC was to move away from controlling credit through quantitative and/or qualitative controls and instead focus upon the rate of growth of the money stock, with a greater role for the Bank Rate.[11] From 13 October 1972, the Bank Rate itself was replaced by the Minimum Lending Rate. As the MLR was automatically linked to the Treasury Bill rate, it was more closely determined by the market than the Bank Rate. Interest rates increased

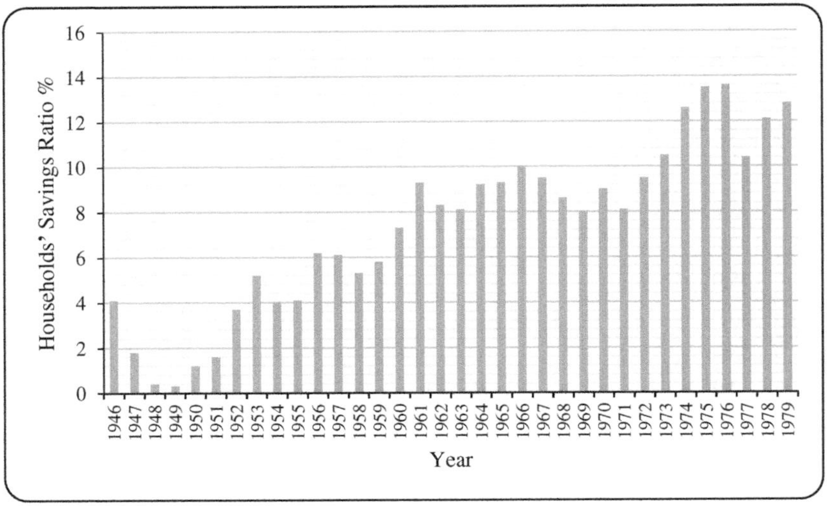

Fig. 3.10 Households' savings ratio, 1946–1979 (*Source* "Research Datasets: A Millennium of Macroeconomic Data, A57: Household Saving, Income And Wealth," *Bank of England*, accessed 24 July 2018, http://www.bankofengland.co.uk/research/Pages/datasets/default.aspx. The Households' savings ratio time series is derived from J. Sefton and M. Weale, *The Reconciliation of National Income and Expenditure: Balanced Estimates of United Kingdom National Accounts, 1920–1990* [London: Cambridge University Press, 1995])

rapidly over the second half of 1973 from 7.5% on 25 June 1973 to 13% on 13 November 1973.[12] Significant amounts of the new credit had funded property development in the early 1970s, but in the second half of 1973 property prices began to fall. In December the secondary banking crisis began to crystallize.[13]

3.2 Financial Repression and Bank Regulation

The literature has tended to argue that the nature of clearing bank regulation was shaped primarily by a desire to minimize the cost of government borrowing, hence the period until the early 1970s is referred to as the period of financial repression. It has given less prominence to the UK's obligation to maintain the value and stability of the pound sterling (which in practice meant maintaining the currency at its par value in relation to the US dollar) as a key factor shaping the nature of clearing bank regulation in the period up until June 1972. It is argued here that the rationale behind the approach to bank regulation adopted is best understood in the context of that obligation. Why was the value and stability of the pound so central to the nature of clearing bank regulation?

First, there was the fact that the UK had an obligation under an international agreement to maintain the value of the pound and the banking system was an instrument through which that could be fulfilled. The United Nations Monetary and Financial Conference at Bretton Woods, New Hampshire, from 1 to 22 July 1944 had set out proposals for the establishment of an IMF) and an International Bank of Reconstruction and Development (IBRD). Forty-four nations were represented. The Articles of Agreement of the IMF established a par value for each participating currency in relation to gold or the US dollar. Under the Agreement, the exchange rate for spot transactions in those currencies could not vary by more than 1% from the par values established at Bretton Woods. The purpose of this requirement was to support stability in exchange rates, and each member of the Fund was bound by a solemn obligation: "Each member undertakes to collaborate with the Fund to promote exchange stability, to maintain orderly exchange arrangements with other members, and to avoid competitive exchange alterations." In certain circumstances, as a last resort, par values could be changed: a member could propose to the Fund a change in the par value of its currency to "correct a fundamental disequilibrium."[14] This obligation under the Articles of Agreement was a fundamental constraint on UK economic policy for the following quarter of a century. British governments (and governments of other members of the Fund) had to pay much closer attention to maintaining the balance of payments on current account and to avoiding current account deficits—especially large and recurrent ones—than would be the case under a system of floating exchange rates. Under a floating exchange rate, regime sterling would tend to depreciate naturally in response to large and recurrent current account deficits. A weaker sterling would encourage exports, thereby bringing imports and exports back into balance, albeit after a time lag. Under the fixed-but-adjustable exchange rate regime established at Bretton Woods, it was not possible to allow sterling to depreciate. Potentially, any current account deficits would require funding from the country's foreign exchange reserves. The position on the current account thus influenced the nature and timing of regulatory interventions in the banking system because the authorities responded to imbalances in the balance of payments on current transactions by restricting domestic credit through the clearing banking system, the logic being that restricting credit would dampen domestic consumption, which in turn would reduce imports. The current balance was in deficit on six occasions between 1946 and 1972 and in the public mind, the nineteen-sixties are often associated with balance of payments crises (four of the six deficits were in that decade). However, following the floating of the pound sterling in June 1972, the position deteriorated dramatically and there were deficits every year for five consecutive years between 1973 and 1977 inclusive. In 1974 alone, the current deficit was £3317 million, which was greater than the cumulative net surplus of £2986 million from 1946 to 1973. In the 1970s, the shift in the focus of economic policy to controlling inflation meant that the focus of bank regulation shifted from controlling credit (in order to manage the balance of payments on current account) to controlling deposits (as bank deposits were a constituent of the money supply). This led to the development and deployment of regulatory techniques such as the Supplementary Special Deposits Scheme, referred to in Chapter 2.

Second, maintaining the value and stability of sterling was seen as necessary to restore and then maintain London as a pre-eminent international financial centre. The City's position as an international financial centre was inextricably tied to confidence in sterling and such confidence depended upon sterling's stability, all the more important given that sterling was a reserve currency. As a reserve currency the pound had several functions: it was held by other countries' central banks and financial institutions; it was widely used in international trade transactions; it was the currency of the sterling area; and finally, many domestic and overseas financial institutions held British government bonds denominated in sterling because of its status as a reserve currency. From the perspective of this second factor, a devaluation of the pound sterling was to be avoided at all costs since a devaluation was the ultimate sign of an unstable and weak currency. There was however an inherent tension between the two objectives described. A strong pound (required to maintain the City as a pre-eminent international financial centre) meant that exports from the UK were expensive and made it more difficult to maintain the current account in balance.

During the period from the inception of the IMF until the pound floated in June 1972 a currency devaluation of sterling occurred twice. In September 1949 a large devaluation of 30.5% from £4.03 to £2.80

occurred, indicating that the par value agreed at the Bretton Woods conference had been unsustainable. Then, in November 1967, a devaluation of the currency from £2.80 to £2.40 (14.3%) took place. Both devaluations occurred under Labour governments and Kynaston observes that Prime Minister Harold Wilson's reluctance to devalue the pound in 1967 should be seen in the context of his involvement in the devaluation decision in 1949. "The very fact of devaluation," he writes, "inevitably had powerful connotations of volte-face and humiliation. These were not connotations that any political party would want to be associated with twice in living memory."[15] The reserve role of sterling came to an end with the 1967 devaluation.[16] The approach to bank regulation adopted in this period needs to be understood in the context of the obligation to maintain the par value of sterling.

3.3 The Consequences of the Approach to Bank Regulation

Stability is ubiquitous as a guiding concept for financial and banking system regulators.[17] The period from the end of the Second World War until the secondary banking crisis was a period of stability in banking in the UK. This is not contested in the literature. The direction of causality is however not clear-cut. Stability was an outcome of the approach to regulation, but may also have enabled and encouraged the approach to regulation adopted. That notwithstanding, it is difficult to avoid the conclusion that the regulation of the clearing banks in this period was highly effective, from the point of view of banking system stability. On the other hand, it also worth exploring whether stability in clearing banking had other, more negative consequences, including ones which were unanticipated.[18] One possibility is that a highly regulated clearing banking system led to regulatory neglect in other parts the banking system. These other parts were more lightly regulated because they fell outside of the most important regulatory perimeter—that around the clearing banks and other high-status banks. Furthermore, the existence of these less-regulated banks may have contributed to the secondary banking crisis. A second possible negative consequence is that stability in clearing banking was achieved at the direct expense of competition in banking and the absence of competition was damaging to clearing banking for the reasons suggested in the literature, as outlined in Chapter 1.

On the first of these potential consequences, as was seen in the previous chapter there was no single regulatory perimeter around the UK banking system in its entirety. There were several definitions of a bank and, as a consequence, multiple versions of the regulatory perimeter. For example, there was a regulatory perimeter around those banks for whom the Bank of England was the direct regulator, such as the London clearing banks and the merchant banks belonging to the Accepting Houses Committee. There was a more extensive but overlapping regulatory perimeter around those high-status banks authorized under the Exchange Control Act 1947 to deal in foreign exchange transactions. Yet another definition would have positioned the regulatory perimeter around those banks certificated by the Board of Trade as banks under the Companies Act 1967. While it is not correct to suggest that sectors of the banking system were completely unregulated, responsibility for regulating banking was somewhat dispersed with HM Treasury, the Bank of England, the Board of Trade and the Board of the Inland Revenue all assuming regulatory and/or supervisory roles of one kind or another. It was not until 1979 that all recognized banks and deposit-taking institutions came under a single Bank of England supervisory umbrella. What is more significant is the fact that it was the Board of Trade, rather than the Bank of England, which came to play an increasingly extensive role in bank regulation. Even so, the Board did not see itself as a supervisor of financial institutions, per se. Its role was more one of certificating, recognizing and/or giving exemptions. The very extensive role of the Board of Trade was a weakness in the regulatory framework. The banking crisis which broke in December 1973, centred upon a group of banks known as the secondary or fringe banks. Of the twenty-six institutions which were supported during the support operation (named “Lifeboat”), eighteen were certificated as banks by the Board of Trade under Section 123 of the Companies Act 1967, and a further five under Section 127 of that Act. It should be noted, however, that with CCC in 1971—well before the crisis broke in December 1973—the authorities had already begun to blur the distinction between clearing banks and other types of bank and thus to reposition the regulatory perimeter. Under CCC, all banks were to be subject to the new reserve ratio, and any calls for Special Deposits were to be at the same rate for all banks. The cash and liquidity ratio—to which only the clearing banks had been subject—were eliminated. There was thus a significant reconfiguration of the regulatory perimeter well before December 1973.

In addition to less-regulated types of bank, there were money and capital markets (notably the euromarkets) which lay outside the most important regulatory perimeter to the extent that these funds were deposited outside the primary banking sector banks. These markets were therefore a source of potential instability.[19] The eurodollar market had emerged in 1955 and the eurobond market in 1963. Michie estimates that by 1968, 60% of eurobond trading was taking place in London.[20] By 1978 the net size of the eurocurrency market was some $375 billion.[21] According to Schooner and Taylor, the euromarkets provided "the liquidity and wholesale market funds to spur the growth of an unregulated domestic banking sector [...] outside the Bank's traditional sphere of influence, or indeed interest."[22] While it could be argued that these markets contributed to the secondary banking crisis, it needs to be borne in mind that the secondary banking crisis occurred two years and two months *after* a major change to the post-war regulatory framework. The framework which prevailed from 1946 had ended in 1971 with the new policy of CCC. Among other things CCC was intended to address the problem of the secondary banks; the authorities were convinced that by unshackling the London clearing banks, many of the weaker and less efficient secondary banks would be driven out of business but that did not happen until the crisis itself. Furthermore, it should be borne in mind that the secondary banking crisis was a relatively small scale crisis which did not spread to the primary banking sector and to that extent the regulatory framework prevented contagion. Reid estimates that the Bank of England and the clearing banks provided around £1300 million of support to the secondary banks during the crisis, with *actual* costs incurred being in the region of a relatively modest £150 million.[23]

Was stability in clearing bank achieved at the cost of competition in banking? The dominant interpretation of clearing banking in this period assumes that this was the case. In doing so, it assumes that there is a trade-off between stability and competition, thus implicitly accepting what is sometimes referred to as the competition-fragility hypothesis. The empirical evidence as to the relationship between competition and stability in banking is however not conclusive. In an early seminal contribution to the development of the competition-fragility hypothesis, Keeley argued that "anticompetitive restrictions [...] made bank charters valuable."[24] The charter value, which is the ratio of the market value of a bank's assets to their book value, emanates from the fact that there are entry restrictions into banking. Any charter value is eliminated in the event of bankruptcy so banks have a strong incentive to avoid bankruptcy by not taking excessive risks. The charter value thus works as a counterweight excessive risk-taking. The erosion of a bank's charter value through liberalization—for example, the relaxation of restrictions over state branching in the United States—removes that incentive. The risk profile of a bank increases accordingly. There is thus a trade-off between competition and stability, the essence of the competition-fragility hypothesis. In his historical overview, Gorton assumes a form of the competition-fragility hypothesis, arguing that the reason for the absence of financial crises in the United States between 1934 and 2007 was that banks were able to earn monopoly profits on account of high charter values and the lack of "invasive innovation."[25] In recent empirical studies, Vives and Beck, De Jonghe and Schepens have advanced versions of the competition-fragility hypothesis.[26]

On the other hand, a number of studies have questioned the competition-fragility hypothesis and have supported instead the competition-stability hypothesis. They have also contributed to a body of empirical evidence that suggests that concentration in banking per se does not undermine stability, and that concentration is not necessarily a good proxy for the absence of competition. Concentrated banking systems it is argued tend to be stable and a concentrated banking system is not necessarily one from which competition is absent. It should be noted at this point that there is a general tendency for banking systems to be concentrated. The OECD has observed that "banking systems in many countries display oligopolistic structures, but the structure does not necessarily mean they do not lead to competitive outcomes."[27] Clearing banking in the UK in the period of this research was no exception being a collusive oligopoly. Studies which lend support to the competition-stability hypothesis include: Claessens and Laeven; Boyd, De Nicolò and Jalal; Beck, Demirgüç-Kunt and Levine; Berger, Klapper and Turk-Ariss; and Anginer, Demirgüç-Kunt and Zhu.[28] If this hypothesis is correct, it leads to the question of how concentrated was clearing banking? During the period 1946–1966 clearing banking was moderately concentrated. The level of concentration in banking was fairly static from 1946 until 1970, although it did increase slightly in the 1960s. The merger of two of the Big Five—Westminster Bank and National Provincial—in 1968 increased concentration and deposits with the three largest deposit-taking banks (Barclays, NatWest and Midland) accounted for 78% of all deposits held by the London clearing banks after that merger.[29]

From 1970, in contrast, there is a very marked decline in the degree of concentration. As has been seen, it was the 1970s that banking became less stable. It is instructive to place concentration in the post-war period in a slightly longer-term perspective. de-Ramon and Straughan's study of UK deposit-taking institutions over the period 1989–2013 shows that the Herfindahl-Hirschman Index (HHI) based on total assets increased over that period and stood at 1887 by the first half of 2010. This was higher than concentration in clearing banking at any point over the period 1946–1966, albeit that the category "deposit-taking institutions" used in their study is much broader than the category "London clearing banks," with 127 deposit-taking institutions included in de-Ramon and Straughan's dataset.[30] Given that this later period has been less stable, this study calls into question the idea that concentrated banking systems tend to be stable.

A critical question when measuring the degree of concentration and/or competition in banking is how the "industry" being measured is to be defined. Should the industry be defined on an entity basis, or on an activity (or functional) basis? With clearing banking, for example, there were eleven London clearing banks and the clearing banking industry could be narrowly defined as those eleven banks. On the other hand, what about the banks for whom the London clearing banks acted as agents—were they also part of the clearing banking industry? Is it correct to include all eleven clearing banks, or is competition better measured with respect to the Big Five clearing banks only? Alternatively, should an evaluation of competition be based on function? For example, a core function of the London clearing banks was the provision of deposit accounts to the public. Is the industry definition therefore all those financial institutions offering deposit accounts to the public? The clearing banks also made loans and advances, so would the relevant industry unit of analysis be the entire population of institutions providing loans and advances? If so, the boundary would extend well beyond the London clearing banks and would include, for example, the finance houses. Much of the empirical research adopts the entity approach by identifying a group, or type, of bank and then evaluating competition within that group. Adopting the entity approach may have led to too much emphasis in the historiography on the fact that there were a very small number of London clearing banks and inferring from this that competition was absent. This is inconsistent with the fact that barriers into the activity of deposit-taking were not high, as is evidenced by the number of overseas and foreign banks locating in the City in the 1960s, many of whom took deposits, albeit mainly from commercial rather than retail customers. Furthermore, there were numerous substitute products and services for those with savings.

In evaluating competition in banking it needs to be borne in mind that the structure of banking and financial services in this period was not static. There was growth across a wide range of financial institutions during the period under review. Watson analysed changes in assets of types of UK financial institution over the period 1955 until 2000 and a slightly modified version of her data is reproduced in Table 3.1.[31]

The assets of all types of financial institution grew strongly between 1955 and 1975. In the case of banks (including the non-clearing banks), their assets grew by a factor of 14 over that period, for insurance by a factor of 16, and for pension funds by a factor of 7.[32] The rate of growth across all types of bank and financial institution exploded in the 1970s. The assets of the London clearing banks as a percentage of the total assets of UK financial institutions fell from 47.8% in 1955 to 17.3% in 1975. In terms of the types of asset represented on the balance sheets of the London clearings banks, there was a trend for investment assets to be replaced with assets in the form of loans and advances. This change increased the London clearing banks' exposure to risk given that generally, loans are riskier assets than investments. This is particularly the case given that the clearing banks tended to hold the lowest risk investments anyway, such as UK Treasury Bills and UK government bonds. In the market for savings, the London clearing banks were losing market share to building societies, pension funds and life assurance companies over the period from 1950 to 1971. A picture thus emerges of a banking and financial services sector which grew strongly in the twenty-five to thirty years after the Second World War particularly from the late 1960s onwards, but one in which the London clearing banks were denuded of their dominant position in the sector.

Alongside the changing structure of the banking and financial services sector, there was a narrative which became increasingly vociferous during the 1960s that clearing banking was uncompetitive. This narrative held that the clearing banks were inefficient, undynamic and disinclined to be innovative and was evident in a number of quarters, including the press. The *Times* commented in January 1969: "The British Clearing Banks, which have come under relentless public scrutiny in the past two years for their restrictions on competition against each other, have once again

Table 3.1 Assets of UK financial institutions, 1955–2000 (£ million current prices)

Year	*Banking sector*	*Of which: London clearing banks*	*Building societies*	*Insurance (long-term and general)*	*Pension funds*	*Investment trusts*	*Unit trusts*	*Total Assets*	*Banking sector assets as percentage of total assets*	*London clearing banks as a percentage of total assets*
1955	7905	6792	2075	1750	1870	620		14,220	55.6	47.8
1958	10,370	7300	2620	5990	2500	710	90	22,280	46.5	32.8
1960		8110	3183	4820		1989	191	–	–	–
1965	15,808	10,390	5577	9867	5380	3119	500	40,251	39.3	25.8
1970	33,727	11,410	10,940	15,452	7644	4469	1316	73,548	45.9	15.5
1975	107,682	31,501	24,364	27,890	13,589	5651	2537	181,713	59.3	17.3
1980	233,392	63,452	54,317	65,262	51,555	8352	4629	417,507	55.9	15.2
1985	589,880		121,239	157,239	156,395	18,085	18,433	1,061,271	55.6	
1990	1,031,245		221,974	276,530	302,670	19,108	41,617	1,893,144	54.5	
1995	1,476,769		297,294	553,020	519,270	43,062	104,069	2,993,484	49.3	
2000	1,467,943		158,703	1,021,711	765,199	60,499	222,824	3,696,879	39.7	

Sources For all years except 1958: Katherine Watson, "The Financial Services Sector Since 1945," in ***The Cambridge Economic History of Modern Britain Volume 3: Structural Change and Growth, 1939–2000***, ed. Roderick Floud and Paul Johnson (Cambridge: Cambridge University Press, March 2008), accessed 19 September 2017, http://www.cambridge.org/core, Table 7.1. Watson collects her data for 1955 from the CSO evidence to the Radcliffe Committee in Volume 1, part III and for other years from ***Financial Statistics***. For 1958: Committee on the Working of the Monetary System, ***Report***, Cmnd. 827, August 1959, to face page 360, para. 127, Table 20, column headed 'End 1958'. The final two columns on the right are calculated by the author. The other data in the London clearing banks column is from: David K. Shephard, ***The Growth and Role of UK Financial Institutions 1880–1962*** (London: Methuen & Co Ltd., 1971), Table (A) 1.8 London Clearing Banks, End-of-Year Consolidated Balance Sheet 1919–1966 (Assets and liabilities £ millions); ***Annual Abstract of Statistics No. 112 1975***, Table 390; and ***Bank of England Quarterly Bulletins*** Quarter 4 1976 and Quarter 4 1981. By 1985, assets of the London clearing banks were not given separately in the Bank of England Quarterly Bulletins left themselves open for criticism in publishing profit figures which strain credulity."[33] The *Economist* contrasted British banking unfavourably with banking in Canada (where greater competition had been introduced in May 1967), and Australia where banks operated "within conditions of truly effective competition" whereas in the UK, "the banks grow bigger and fewer, and effective competition between them gets less and less chance."[34] Criticism of clearing banks also emerged from the think tank the Institute of Economic Affairs, who, in their 1970 pamphlet *Competition in Banking*, anticipated many of the changes introduced with CCC in 1971.[35] There was also criticism from the public although it should be acknowledged that public criticism of banks was not a new phenomenon. Newton explores the sources of public and political criticisms of banking in the 1930s and how the banks responded to these.[36] The Institute of Bankers' Prize Essay Competition for 1957–1958 was on the topic of: "The banks are frequently criticized in certain sections of the press: prepare a reasoned reply, showing how much the country owes to a soundly based banking system."[37] In 1966, conscious of their poor public image, the CLCB discussed engaging a firm of public relations consultants to advise them "what might be done to improve the attitude of the public to banking."[38] Criticism of banks and bankers has of course been particularly intense since the global financial crisis.[39]

Notwithstanding this narrative, there is considerable evidence of product, process, marketing, organizational and management innovation in clearing banking during this period. For example, personal loans were introduced by Midland in 1958; a credit transfer "giro" system was implemented by the clearing banks collectively in 1960; the cheque card was launched by National Provincial in 1965; the credit card by Barclays in 1966; the cash dispenser by Barclays in 1967; and in the period 1966–1970, Lloyds computerized its entire branch network, linking the branches to its Computer Centres, to name but a few innovations. In any case, the authorities continued to have reservations about introducing more competition into banking. The authorities tolerated the cartel—which in many respects worked in their (the authorities') interests—but views about cartels were changing. Fear observes that, before 1945, "most of the world thought that cartels brought widespread benefits [...] cartels do not abolish competition, but regulate it."[40] Even in the immediate post-war period cartels were seen as a way of regulating competition in order to reduce the risk of a post-war slump. In return for being permitted to operate through cartels, industry would support government economic policy.[41] Into the second half of the century, however, antitrust ideas began to disseminate throughout the world.[42] Wilks posits that, by the mid-1960s, most cartel agreements had been eliminated.[43] There was a growing sense by the late 1960s that the cartel arrangements in clearing banking were anachronistic. The authorities' reservations about competition in banking also reflected a more general tension at the time between the requirements of competition policy on the one hand (which would seek to control mergers and monopoly) and the requirements of industrial policy on the other (which would tend be more tolerant of mergers). Given that a monopoly did not exist in clearing banking and no mergers between the Big Five had occurred between 1918 and 1968, the target of most criticism from a competition policy point of view was bank restrictive practices. The practice of collective pricing was seen to facilitate high levels of dividends and profits. When the government referred clearing bank charges to the NBPI in June 1966, its stated reason for doing so was that the "profit and dividend record" of most banks had increased substantially in recent years.[44] High profits were, moreover, indirect evidence that the clearing banks were not innovative enough. The *Economist*, singling out Lloyds Bank, set out the causal connection thus: "innovations do not pay – or anyway not immediately. That is suggested by the greater profitability of Lloyds on almost any fair basis of comparison; it is usually reckoned the staidest of the big four."[45] However, the NBPI recognized that it was the generally higher levels of the Bank Rate during the 1960s which had contributed greatly to increased profit margins.[46] Between 1950 and 1959 the Bank Rate ranged from 2.5 to 7%, while between 1960 and 1969 it was in the range 4–8%. Capie and Billings analysed bank profitability over the period 1920–1970 and found that returns on capital showed a very shallow "U-shape" over that period, indicating that profits were rising into the 1960s and 1970s, albeit modestly.[47] Over the period 1946–1979 the dividend paid by Midland was never below 10% of paid-up share capital and, except for in the 1970s, was within the range 14–19%.[48] There was also public dissatisfaction about the restrictive practice of uniform bank opening hours. While uniform opening hours blunted competition *between* the clearing banks, it increased the threat of substitute products and services. The *Times*, reporting on a survey carried out on behalf of the London and Scottish clearing banks, identified bank opening hours as their "main weakness" in competition with the Post Office.[49]

Perfect competition exists where firms are price takers and where there is freedom of entry and exit into an industry. The clearing banks were not price takers (they were able to set prices, in some cases collectively through the CLCB) so, by that measure, clearing banking was not perfectly competitive. Moreover, barriers to entry into clearing banking were generally high. Rivalry between the clearing banks was muted and restrictive practices were tolerated. On the other hand, although the market was moderately concentrated, there is evidence that the market was contestable. There was not a monopoly in banking and there were no mergers between the Big Five banks until 1968. If the market is defined from a functional rather than an entity point of view, there were a growing number of substitute products and services to compete directly with clearing bank products and services. Moreover, concentration in clearing banking did not lead to excessive bank charges, according to the report of the NBPI. Finally, it is not the case that under conditions of moderated competition the banks did not innovate.

Chapter 1 explored the nature of clearing bank regulation and this chapter has considered the economic and industry context within which clearing banking operated. To conclude this chapter, it is proposed that there were a range of factors which stabilized clearing banking in this period. These stabilizing factors can be thought of as regulatory, institutional and structural counterweights to excessive risk-taking. They are summarized in Table 3.2 and explored further in the section which follows.

Risk is the measurable uncertainty facing a bank and a key role of a bank's board is to manage risk. Risk can be managed in a number of ways: it can be transferred (normally by insuring it); it can be mitigated; it can be accepted; or it can be avoided. In the public mind, the clearing banks were the quintessential risk-averse financial institution. In his 1962 book *Anatomy of Britain*, Anthony Sampson summed up this public perception thus: "In their dedication, their lack of greed, and their sense of quiet service, the joint stock bankers provide a placid, safe centre to financial Britain: one can no more imagine a bank going bust than the monarchy falling."[50] The following section identifies and explains the main risks facing the clearing banks and illustrates the regulatory, institutional and structural counterweights to excessive risk-taking by banks.[51] These counterweights worked against the tendency of individual banks to accept excessive risk, but also worked to thwart the growth of systemic risk. They thus supported the stability of the banking system.

Table 3.2 Counterweights to risks faced by the London clearing banks

Counterweight	*Type of counterweight*	*Principal type(s) of risk mitigated or avoided*
The custom of overdraft lending (as opposed to lending for a specific term—term lending). From the late 1950s onwards, beginning with the Midland, the clearing banks began making term loans	Institutional	Liquidity
The "gentleman's agreement" among the Big Five until 1968 that they would not amalgamate	Institutional	Systemic
The convention of a cash ratio of 8% until 1971	Regulatory	(i) Liquidity (ii) Risk of a bank run
The convention of a liquidity ratio of 28–30% until 1971	Regulatory	(i) Liquidity (ii) Risk of a bank run
The absence of deposit insurance until 1979	Regulatory	Systemic
The system of fixed-but-adjustable exchange rates until 1972 and limited convertibility of currency until 1979	Institutional/structural	(i) Market (exchange rate) (ii) Operational
The tradition of specialization in banking	Institutional	Systemic
The tradition of a uniform spread between the Bank Rate and the interest rate paid on deposits of 2%	Institutional	(i) Systemic (ii) Credit (iii) Market (interest rate)
The tradition of uniform pricing by the London clearing banks (and others) until 1971	Institutional	(i) Systemic (ii) Credit (iii) Market (interest rate)
The custom of placing surplus cash on the discount market	Institutional	Liquidity
Concentration in clearing banking	Regulatory/structural	Systemic

Liquidity risk is a risk which crystallizes when a bank is unable to meet its obligations as they fall due. It arises out of a mismatch between the size and maturity of its assets and liabilities. One type of liquidity risk very specific to banks is the risk of a run on the bank. During the post-war decades, liquidity risk was mitigated in four ways. First, there was the self-regulatory convention of adhering to a liquidity ratio. This required the clearing banks to retain the equivalent of 30% (28% from 1963) of total deposits in the form of liquid assets. In addition, the cash ratio (also a conventional ratio) acted as a counterweight to liquidity risk, and to bank run risk specifically, because it required that on a daily basis the clearing banks held the equivalent of 8% of their total deposits in the most liquid form of all—cash. A further defence against liquidity risk was the fact that traditionally, the London clearing banks lent in the form of overdraft lending, a very low risk form of lending compared with term lending. Overdraft lending reduced the maturity mismatch between bank lending and bank borrowing as both lending and borrowing were short-term. Moreover, in the context of restrictions over credit in which the demand for credit greatly exceeded the supply, lower risk loans would be favoured over riskier ones, all other things equal. The low risk nature of their loans and advances is evidenced by the level of bad debt write-offs by the clearing banks. In the 1960s and 1970s, the clearing banks began to move into the field of term lending. Lloyds Bank, for example, began offering home loans (by nature, very long-term) in 1979. This shift represented a profound change in their business model and increased their exposure to liquidity risk.

Finally, the discount market played a role in maintaining the liquidity of the financial system as a whole. The Discount Houses absorbed any short-term cash surpluses from the London clearing banks and utilized these surpluses by buying bills, most notably Treasury Bills. Money at call on the discount market was a highly liquid asset, and could be included in the calculation of the liquidity ratio. Lending by the London clearing banks to the discount market was also risk-free since the Bank of England was the lender of last resort to the Discount Houses. This market thus helped maintain high levels of liquidity in the financial system and was a counterweight to the crystallization of systemic liquidity risk.

Default (or credit, or counterparty) risk is the risk that "a bank borrower or counterparty will fail to meet its obligations in accordance with agreed terms."[52] Default risk was not a significant risk to the clearing banks until 1971 because the availability of credit was restricted. Given that the demand for credit exceeded the supply, any lending by the clearing banks tended to be lent to high-quality counterparties who were not at risk of defaulting. The restriction of credit was largely implemented through extra-legal techniques such as quantitative controls over lending. As a result, the clearing banks experienced very low levels of bad debts. The chair of Lloyds remarked in 1954—almost sheepishly—that "It is true that our bad debts in recent years have been small."[53] It is also evident in reports to the board of Lloyds Bank in the 1950s and into the

1960s from its districts. In 1955 for example, the Eastern Counties Area reported that bad debts (of £6317) as a percentage of net profit stood at 0.91%.[54] While default risk was largely avoided by the clearing banks, it could be argued that it was transferred to other financial institutions such as the hire purchase companies and secondary banks. Demand for credit was growing and if consumers were unable to obtain credit from the clearing banks they would seek it elsewhere. There was thus a transference of default risk to other financial institutions.

The practice of setting uniform prices on deposit accounts, and the relatively fixed and stable spread between the rate at which they lent and the rate paid on deposit accounts, helped sustain and increase the profitability of clearing banking over the period 1940–1968.[55] This meant that banks were not under pressure to lower their lending standards to maintain their profit margins. Important changes in the 1970s provided new opportunities for lending. These changes included CCC in 1971; the ending of fixed-but-adjustable exchange rates (between 1971 and 1973); the UK's accession to the European Economic Community on 1 January 1973; the injection of large quantities of petrodollars into the banking system following the oil price shock (1973–1974); and the growing strategic desire of the London clearing banks to transform themselves from international banks into global banks. The clearing banks responded to these opportunities by accepting greater default risk.

Market risk is the risk that there will be losses arising from fluctuations in the value of (or income from) assets, or from fluctuations in interest or exchange rates. The three key market risks facing the clearing banks arose from: fluctuations in the value of British government securities ("gilts"), fluctuations in exchange rates and fluctuations in interest rates.[56] The banks were large holders of gilts. These holdings were assets on their balance sheets. The risk of these assets falling in value was mitigated by a convention that the Bank of England would buy gilts from the banks on request. This practice was discontinued in 1971 with the new policy of CCC, although the Bank did continue to buy stocks on request which had less than one year to maturity. In the period until 1971, there was a general decline in assets in the form of investments. While the decline in investments reduced their market risk, investments were replaced by advances, thus increasing their credit risk.

A specific market risk is exchange rate or currency risk. This risk crystallizes when exchange rate fluctuations affect the value of a bank's assets and liabilities. Institutional features of the international economy helped mitigate exchange rate risk until the early 1970s in two ways. First, there was the fact that exchange rates for most major currencies were fixed-but-adjustable under the Articles of Agreement of the IMF. The signatories to the Agreement had an obligation to ensure that the value of their currency for spot exchange transactions was maintained at a value within 1% of the currency's par value. There was therefore very little volatility in exchange rates. The banks were unconvinced of the merits of floating exchange rates in the period after the war; the chair of Lloyds Bank Lord Balfour of Burleigh opined in 1950 that to float the pound would be "setting sterling adrift to weather the buffetings of supply and demand."[57] This fixed-but-adjustable system of exchange rates disintegrated between 1971 and 1973 when many major currencies moved to floating rates. Floating exchange rates between major currencies presented opportunities for speculative currency trading and it thus became possible for the clearing banks to accept much greater exchange rate risk. In the case of Lloyds Bank International Limited (LBI, a subsidiary of Lloyds Bank) exchange rate risk crystallized in 1974 when LBI experienced losses of £33 million (around £28 million after insurance) after staff at its Lugano branch took out unauthorized and uncovered foreign exchange positions. The losses had a significant impact on Lloyds Bank's performance in 1974: its profit before taxation in that year was £74.9 million compared with £130.7 million in the previous year. The Annual Report for 1974 explained that the loss had taken place "against a background of sharp fluctuations in currency values following the introduction of floating rates of exchange."[58] The second institutional feature was exchange control. Exchange rate risk can only crystallize when it is permissible to convert one currency into another. Although the ability to convert sterling into other currencies after the Second World War was subject to control under the Exchange Control Act 1947, signatories to the IMF's Articles of Agreement were obliged to work towards the convertibility of their currencies for current account transactions. In 1958 convertibility was introduced in relation to the western European currencies for current account purposes. In 1979 the newly elected Conservative government abolished all remaining exchange controls and it became much easier for banks to accept greater currency risk.

Interest rate risk, another form of market risk, was mitigated by the clearing banks' practice of collectively agreeing the rate of interest payable on deposit accounts, typically at a rate of 2% below Bank Rate. The rate of interest receivable on their lending also tended to be set in relation to the Bank Rate. This meant that interest rate "spreads" were stable. One consequence of CCC in 1971 (which ended the practice of collective pricing) was that bank spreads decreased significantly. Goodhart pinpoints this as an important unanticipated consequence of CCC: "What we had not foreseen, when introducing C&CC, was that, in the pursuit of expansion and a competitive increase in each of their market shares, the clearing banks would narrow their spreads, i.e. bid up for deposit funds, while keeping lending rates down to attract business."[59]

Operational risk is "the risk of loss resulting from inadequate or failed internal processes, people and systems or from external events."[60] Schenk points to the losses at Lloyds in 1974 on account of the "rogue trader" at the Lugano branch, as an example of the crystallization of operational risk.[61] The loss at Lugano thus involved both currency risk and operational risk. The regulatory, institutional and structural counterweights to operational risk were less in evidence than for liquidity, default and market risk. In fact, there were structural factors which may have encouraged risk-taking. For example, one important way in which to manage the risk of fraud (an operational risk) is to have recruitment procedures which reduce the risk of employing someone who might be motivated to behave fraudulently. In the post-war period the UK economy was operating at close to full employment and the recruitment and retention of staff was a constant operational problem—indeed, it was a major driver behind the introduction of cash dispensers and Automated Teller Machines in the late 1960s and early 1970s, the ATM being "the chief alternative to the human teller during the 1980s."[62] Full employment increased operational risk because it meant that banks might either be short of staff or may have employed staff without the right skills or qualifications. The banks' collective agreement on uniform opening hours went some way to help them to manage this particular risk as it limited the hours which banks were open and from July 1969 they ceased to open on Saturday morning. Operational risks also include risks relating to systems. Once the banks began to computerize their operations from the mid-1960s, managing the risk of a systems failure assumed great importance.

The above risks are risks faced by individual banks. There is also, from the regulator's point of view, the question of the management of systemic risk.[63] One source of systemic risk is the presence of large banks including ones which are so large they are "too big to fail" (TBTF). In a study covering 1250 banks (of whom 137 were large banks with assets of at least $50 billion) Laeven, Ratnovski and Tong found that "large banks, on average, create more individual and systemic risk than smaller banks" and that "regulatory policy needs to pay special attention to the role of large banks."[64] The period of their study (from July 2007 until December 2008) is however rather short and covers the early stages of the global financial crisis, so the generalizability of their conclusions would need to be tested further. Three factors worked against the emergence of very large banks in the earlier period. First, the tradition of specialization meant that there was a natural limit to the growth of a financial institution. Each type of banks had specific core functions; for example, clearing banks offered current accounts, deposit accounts and overdraft facilities, whereas the core function of a building society was to offer loans in the form of mortgages. It was unlikely that a specialist bank could grow to be as large as a universal bank or a financial services conglomerate. The tradition of specialization may also have formed an obstacle to interbank lending and borrowing, and the interconnectedness which ensues. Second, the "gentleman's agreement" (from 1918 to 1968) among the Big Five not to amalgamate worked against the development of a TBTF bank. Paradoxically, the fact that a cartel was permitted to exist may have removed banks' incentive to merge. Third, the practice by the London clearing banks of uniform pricing and of having a fixed spread between the Bank Rate and the interest rate paid on deposits of 2%, meant that the clearing banks were not compelled to compete on price. Given their market power, it may have been possible for the Big Five to have driven one or more of the Little Six banks out of the market, through predatory pricing. This did not happen and there were eleven London clearing banks for the entire period from 1935 until 1962, and ten until 1968. Following a number of mergers between 1968 and 1970, the number had reduced to six by 1970.

Systemic risk has a time dimension as it may fluctuate with the business cycle. This type of risk is cyclical (or business cycle) risk. Claessens and Kose observe a connection between the business cycle and banking crises: "Banking panics more likely occur near the peak of the business cycle, with recessions on the horizon, because of concerns that loans do not get repaid."[65] In a similar vein, Akerlof and Shiller suggest that conduct and behaviour are connected to the business cycle. Misconduct tends to occur when opportunities for it increase, and when the incentives for good conduct and behaviour are weak. As they put it, "the business cycle is connected to fluctuations in personal commitment to principles of good behavior and to fluctuations in predatory activity, which in turn is related to changes in opportunities for such activity."[66] They argue that "it is now time to redesign financial regulations to take account of the animal spirits that often drive the markets."[67] While not expressed quite so vividly, there is a strong focus in contemporary regulation on the management of cyclical risk, most notably through the requirement under Basel III for banks to hold countercyclical capital buffers of up to 2.5% of its risk-weighted assets. A bank's capital should be able to fluctuate according to the macroeconomic environment. The intuition behind this is that, as Revell has put it, "At times of increased risk, profits and capital ratios of banks and other credit institutions should be rising."[68] In the next chapter, other aspects of the contemporary approach to bank regulation will be considered and some key points of contrast between the approach to bank regulation in the period under review, and that taken since the global financial crisis 2007–2009, will be identified and explored.

Notes

1. William A. Allen, *Monetary Policy and Financial Repression in Britain, 1951–59* (Basingstoke: Palgrave Macmillan, 2014); J. H. B. Tew, "Monetary Policy Part I," in *British Economic Policy 1960–74*, ed. F. T. Blackaby (Cambridge: Cambridge University Press, 1978); and M. J. Artis, "Monetary Policy Part II," in *British Economic Policy 1960–74*, ed. F. T. Blackaby (Cambridge: Cambridge University Press, 1978).
2. David Aikman, Oliver Bush, and Alan M. Taylor, "Monetary Versus Macroprudential Policies: Causal Impacts of Interest Rates and Credit Controls in the Era of the Radcliffe Report, Working Paper 22380," in *NBER Working Paper Series* (National Bureau of Economic Research, June 2016).
3. Committee on the Working of the Monetary System, *Report*, Cmnd. 827, August 1959, para. 69.
4. For an overview of economic policy developments in the UK since 1939, see Jim Tomlinson, "Economic Policy," in *The Cambridge Economic History of Modern Britain Volume 3: Structural Change and Growth, 1939–2000*, ed. Roderick Floud and Paul Johnson (Cambridge: Cambridge University Press, 2008).
5. The unemployment rate in the UK for the period April–June 2018 to was 4.0%. "Unemployment," *Office for National Statistics*, accessed 24 August 2018, https://www.ons.gov.uk/employmentandlabourmarket/peoplenotinwork/unemployment.
6. "Nixon Ends Convertibility of US Dollars to Gold and Announces Wage/Price Controls, August 1971," *Federal Reserve History*,

accessed 12 July 2018, https://www.federalreservehistory.org/essays/gold_convertibility_ends.

7. Anthony Barber, speech, 9 September 1971, Bishopsgate Institute, Parliamentary Profiles Archive 5/63A: Barber of Wentbridge.
8. "The Smithsonian Agreement, December 1971," *Federal Reserve History*, accessed 12 July 2018, https://www.federalreservehistory.org/essays/smithsonian_agreement?WT.si_n=Search&WT.si_x=3.
9. Jim O'Donoghue, Louise Goulding, and Grahame Allen, "Consumer Price Inflation Since 1750," *Economic Trends 604*, March 2004, 44, Table 2, accessed 16 July 2018, http://webarchive.nationalarchives.gov.uk/20160105160709/, http://ons.gov.uk/ons/rel/elmr/economic-trends--discontinued-/no--604--march-2004/index.html.
10. Central Statistical Office, *Annual Abstract of Statistics No. 119* (London: HMSO, 1983), Table 17.8.
11. "Further Details About Wholesale—Baserate Data," *Bank of England*, accessed 12 July 2018, http://www.bankofengland.co.uk/statistics/pages/iadb/notesiadb/wholesale_baserate.aspx.
12. "Official Bank Rate History Data from 1694: Changes in Bank Rate, Minimum Lending Rate, Minimum Band 1 Dealing Rate, Repo Rate and Official Bank Rate, Historical Since 1694," *Bank of England*, accessed 12 July 2018, https://www.bankofengland.co.uk/monetary-policy/the-interest-rate-bank-rate.
13. See Margaret Reid, "The Dash for Growth—And Its Consequences," in *The Secondary Banking Crisis, 1973–75: Its Causes and Course* (London: Macmillan, 1982): 70–85.
14. "Articles of Agreement: International Monetary Fund and International Bank for Reconstruction and Development," accessed 12 July 2018, https://fraser.stlouisfed.org/files/docs/historical/martin/17_07_19440701.pdf, Article IV, Sections 4 and 5, p. 5.
15. David Kynaston, *Austerity Britain: 1945–1951* (London: Bloomsbury Publishing plc, 2008): 351.
16. Catherine R. Schenk, "Britain in the World Economy," in *A Companion to Contemporary Britain, 1939–2000*, ed. Paul Addison and Harriet Jones (Oxford: Blackwell, 2007): 468.
17. For example, the Financial Stability Board, an international body which coordinates the standard-setting, regulatory and supervisory activities of national and international authorities, has as its core purpose to "promote international financial stability." "About the FSB," *Financial Stability Board*, accessed 24 August 2018, http://www.fsb.org/about/.
18. In a seminal article, Merton explored five reasons why it may not be possible to anticipate the consequences of purposive social actions. Robert K. Merton, "The Unanticipated Consequences of Purposive Social Action," *American Sociological Review* 1, no. 6 (December 1936).

19. The UK banking sector as at the end of 1969 consisted of the following types of banks: deposit banks (including the clearing banks), National Giro, the discount houses belonging to the London Discount Market Association, banks represented on the Accepting Houses Committee, British Overseas and Commonwealth Banks, American Banks in London, Foreign Banks and Affiliates, Japanese Banks in London, other overseas banks, and other banks. See *Bank of England Statistical Abstract Number 1, 1970, Tables 9(I) and 10(4)*, accessed 27 April 2018, https://www.bankofengland.co.uk/-/media/boe/files/archive/statistical-abstract/number-1-1970.pdf. The rapid growth of non-clearing banks is illustrated by the fact that at the end of 1969, the London clearing banks held £10,724 million in current and deposit accounts (up from £7691 million in March 1963) while the American banks in London alone held deposits of £9755 million (up from £564 million in March 1963).
20. Ranald C. Michie, "Suppression, Regulation, and Evasion: 1939–70," in *The Global Securities Market: A History* (Oxford: Oxford University Press, 2006): 246.
21. Committee to Review the Functioning of Financial Institutions, *Report*, Cmnd. 7937, June 1980, para. 62.
22. Heidi Mandanis Schooner and Michael Taylor, "Convergence and Competition: The Case of Bank Regulation in Britain and the United States," *Michigan Journal of International Law* 20, no. 4 (Summer 1999): 623–24.
23. Margaret Reid, *Secondary Banking Crisis, 1973–75: Its Causes and Course* (London: Macmillan, 1982): 190–92. Reid's book was published in 1982, at which point the support operation had not technically been completed. The figures are therefore tentative.
24. Michael C. Keeley, "Deposit Insurance, Risk, and Market Power in Banking," *The American Economic Review* 80, no. 5 (December 1990): 1198.
25. Gary B. Gorton, "The Quiet Period and Its End," in *Misunderstanding Financial Crises: Why We Don't See Them Coming* (New York, NY: Oxford University Press, 2012): 133.
26. Xavier Vives, "Competition and Stability in Banking, WP-852," in *Working Papers* (IESE Business School, University of Navarra, April 2010); Thorsten Beck, Olivier De Jonghe, and Glenn Schepens, "Bank Competition and Stability: Cross-Country Heterogeneity," *Journal of Financial Intermediation* 22, no. 2 (2013), accessed 24 March 2017, http://dx.doi.org/10.1016/j.jfi.2012.07.001. They use the 2008 version of the World Bank's Bank Regulation and Supervision database. This database has been updated since, see James R. Barth, Gerard Caprio Jr., and Ross Levine, "Bank Regulation and Supervision in 180 Countries

from 1999 to 2011, Working Paper 18733," in *NBER Working Paper Series* (National Bureau of Economic Research, January 2013).

27. The Organisation for Economic Co-operation and Development, "Bank Competition and Financial Stability" (OECD Publishing, 2011): 14, accessed 1 August 2018, http://www.oecd.org/daf/fin/financial-markets/48501035.pdf.
28. Stijn Claessens and Luc Laeven, "What Drives Bank Competition? Some International Evidence," *Journal of Money, Credit and Banking* 36, no. 3, Part 2 (2003); John H. Boyd, Gianni De Nicolò, and Abu M. Jalal, "Bank Risk-Taking and Competition Revisited: New Theory and New Evidence, WP/06/297," in *IMF Working Papers* (December 2006); Thorsten Beck, Asli Demirgüç-Kunt, and Ross Levine, "Bank Concentration, Competition, and Crises: First Results," *Journal of Banking & Finance* 30 (2006), accessed 30 March 2017, http://www.sciencedirect.com; Thorsten Beck, Asli Demirgüç-Kunt, and Ross Levine, "Bank Concentration and Crises, Working Paper 9921," in *NBER Working Paper Series* (National Bureau of Economic Research, 2003); Allen N. Berger, Leora F. Klapper, and Rima Turk-Ariss, "Bank Competition and Financial Stability, World Bank Policy Research Working Paper 4696," in *World Bank Policy Research Working Papers* (The World Bank, August 2008); and Deniz Anginer, Asli Demirgüç-Kunt, and Min Zhu, "How Does Bank Competition Affect Systemic Stability? World Bank Policy Working Paper Number 5981," in *World Bank Policy Research Working Papers* (The World Bank, February 2012).
29. "Grouping of Deposits on 17th July 1968," BoE G1/13 Governor's File: Various Bank Mergers and Amalgamations.
30. Sebastian J. A. de-Ramon and Michael Straughan, "Measuring Competition in the UK Deposit-Taking Sector, Staff Working Paper No. 631," in *Staff Working Papers* (London: Bank of England, December 2016): 1, 14–15.
31. Katherine Watson, "The Financial Services Sector Since 1945," in *The Cambridge Economic History of Modern Britain Volume 3: Structural Change and Growth, 1939–2000*, ed. Roderick Floud and Paul Johnson, Cambridge Histories Online (Cambridge: Cambridge University Press, March 2008): Table 7.1.
32. Ibid.
33. "Crosland Must Make the Banks Tell More," *Times*, 22 January 1969, 25, The Times Digital Archive 1785–2010, Gale Cengage Learning.
34. "New World for Canadian Banks," *Economist*, 16 November 1968, 28, The Economist Historical Archive 1843–2012, Gale Cengage Learning.
35. Brian Griffiths, *Competition in Banking* (London: Institute of Economic Affairs, 1970).

36. Lucy Newton, "Government, the Banks and Industry in Inter-War Britain," in *Business and Politics in Europe, 1900–1970*, ed. Terry Gourvish (Cambridge: Cambridge University Press, 2003): 145–68.
37. "Annual General Meeting, 7 May 1958," The Institute of Bankers Minutes of Public Meetings, LMA CLC/B/045/MS30851/002.
38. Minutes of a Meeting of the Chief Executive Officers of the Clearing Banks, 20 January 1966, LMA CLC/B/029/MS32037/017 Committee of London Clearing Bankers and Chief Executive Officers' Committee Minutes (2/7A and 2/7/1). Public image was an issue to which the Committee returned in the 1970s. In 1973–1974 it established a special Public Attitudes Working Party. See Minutes of a Meeting of the Committee of London Clearing Bankers, 7 February 1974, LMA CLC/B/029/MS32037/025. When the Labour Party began seriously to debate taking the major clearing banks and insurance companies into public ownership, the issue assumed a new level of urgency.
39. In October 2016, for example, a highly critical report was published by New City Agenda and Cass Business School, "Cultural Change in the FCA, PRA & Bank of England: Practising What They Preach?" New City Agenda, accessed 24 August 2018, http://newcityagenda.co.uk/wp-content/uploads/2016/10/NCA-Cultural_Change_in_regulators_report.pdf. The report warned that "unless we change the culture of regulators we will be sleep walking into the next financial crisis," 6.
40. Jeffrey Fear, "Cartels," in *The Oxford Handbook of Business History*, ed. Geoffrey G. Jones and Jonathan Zeitlin, Oxford Handbooks Online (Oxford: Oxford University Press, September 2009): 1–2.
41. Rory MacLeod, "The Promise of Full Employment," in *War and Social Change: British Society in the Second World War*, ed. Harold L. Smith (Manchester: Manchester University Press, 1986): 92.
42. Fear, "Cartels," 1.
43. Stephen Wilks, *In the Public Interest: Competition Policy and the Monopolies and Mergers Commission* (Manchester: Manchester University Press, 1999): 37.
44. National Board for Prices and Incomes, Report No. 34, *Bank Charges*, Cmnd. 3292, May 1967, p. 3, para. 1.
45. "Banking for Profit," *Economist*, 8 August 1970, 42, The Economist Historical Archive 1843–2012, Gale Cengage Learning.
46. National Board for Prices and Incomes, Report No. 34, *Bank Charges*, Cmnd. 3292, May 1967, para. 39.
47. Forrest Capie and Mark Billings, "Profitability in English Banking in the Twentieth Century," *European Review of Economic History* 5, no. 3 (2001): 378–85.
48. A. R. Holmes and Edwin Green, *Midland: 150 Years of Banking Business* (London: BT Batsford Ltd., 1986): 334.

49. Anthony Thomas, "Opening Hours Are Banks' Weak Link," *Times*, 16 October 1968, The Times Digital Archive 1785–2010, Gale Cengage Learning.
50. Anthony Sampson, *Anatomy of Britain* (London: Hodder and Stoughton, 1962): 375.
51. Heffernan identifies the main risks specific to banks today as: liquidity, credit, counterparty, settlement, market, capital, operational and sovereign (or political) risk. See Sheila Heffernan, *Modern Banking* (Chichester: Wiley, 2009): 104–12. The important risks in this period were liquidity risk, default risk, market risk, operational risk and systemic risk.
52. "Principles for the Management of Credit Risk," *Bank for International Settlements*, accessed 3 July 2016, http://www.bis.org/publ/bcbs75.htm, para. 2.
53. Lloyds Bank Limited, Statement by the Chairman Accompanying the Report of the Directors and Balance Sheet for the Year Ended 31 December 1954, 7, LBGA HO/S/Rep/10.
54. Report to a Meeting of the Board of Lloyds Bank Limited, 25 May 1956, LBGA HO/D/Boa/Age/26.
55. Capie and Billings, "Profitability in English Banking in the Twentieth Century," Tables 2 and 3.
56. "Standards: Interest Rate Risk in the Banking Book, April 2016," *Bank for International Settlements*, accessed 16 July 2018, http://www.bis.org/bcbs/publ/d368.pdf. Interest Rate Risk in the Banking Book is defined as: "the current or prospective risk to the bank's capital and earnings arising from adverse movements in interest rates that affect the bank's banking book positions. When interest rates change, the present value and timing of future cash flows change. This in turn changes the underlying value of a bank's assets, liabilities and off-balance sheet items and hence its economic value. Changes in interest rates also affect a bank's earnings by altering interest rate-sensitive income and expenses, affecting its net interest income (NII)," 3.
57. Lloyds Bank Limited Report of Directors and Balance Sheet for the Year Ended 31 December 1950, Statement by the Chairman, 5, LBGA HO/S/Rep/9.
58. Lloyds Bank Limited Report and Accounts 1974, Statement by the Chairman, 22, LBGA HO/S/Rep/15–19.
59. Charles A. E. Goodhart, "Competition and Credit Control: Some Personal Reflections," *Financial History Review* 22, no. 2 (2015): 244.
60. "Principles for the Sound Management of Operational Risk—Final Document, June 2011," 3, *Bank for International Settlements*, accessed 16 July 2018, http://www.bis.org/publ/bcbs195.htm.
61. Schenk points to the failure to manage operational risk, failures of enforcement, and problems caused by a dissonance between regulatory

rules and norms as important factors in the loss. Catherine Schenk, "Rogue Trading at Lloyds Bank International, 1974: Operational Risk in Volatile Markets," *Business History Review* 91, no. 1 (2017).

62. Bernardo Bátiz-Lazo, "Emergence and Evolution of ATM Networks in the UK, 1967–2000," *Business History* 51, no. 1 (2009): 16.
63. Jaime Caruana suggests that "Following the work of the IMF, FSB and BIS for the G20, systemic risk can be defined as 'a risk of disruption to financial services that is caused by an impairment of all or parts of the financial system and has the potential to have serious negative consequences for the real economy.'" See "Systemic Risk: How to Deal with It?" *Bank for International Settlements*, February 2010, accessed 24 August 2018, http://www.bis.org/publ/othp08.htm#P01. Systemic risk has two dimensions: a cross-sectional one—how risk is distributed within the system at a point in time—and a time dimension concerned with the accumulation of risk over time and its cyclicality.
64. Luc Laeven, Lev Ratnovski, and Hui Tong, "Bank Size and Systemic Risk, SDN/14/04," in *IMF Staff Discussion Notes* (International Monetary Fund, May 2014): 23, 22.
65. Stijn Claessens and M. Ayhan Kose, "Financial Crises: Explanations, Types, and Implications, WP/13/28," in *IMF Working Papers* (International Monetary Fund, January 2013): 20.
66. George A. Akerlof and Robert Shiller, J., *Animal Spirits: How Human Psychology Drives the Economy and Why It Matters for Global Capitalism*, 9th ed. (Princeton: Princeton University Press, 2009; reprint, 2010): 38.
67. Ibid., 148.
68. J. R. S. Revell, *Costs and Margins in Banking: An International Survey*, ed. Organisation for Economic Co-operation and Development (Paris: Organisation for Economic Co-operation and Development, 1980): 116.

References

Primary Sources

Bank of England Archive

G1/13: Governor's Files: Various Bank Mergers and Amalgamations.

Bishopsgate Institute

Parliamentary Profiles Archive—Lords 5/63A Barber of Wentbridge.

Lloyds Banking Group Archive

HO/S/Rep/8–19.
HO/D/Boa/Age/26–29.

London Metropolitan Archives

MS30851: Chartered Institute of Bankers: Annual General Meetings and Other Public Meeting Minutes.

MS32037: Committee of London Clearing Bankers and Chief Executive Officers' Committee Minutes (2/7a and 2/7/1).

Command Papers

Committee on the Working of the Monetary System, *Report*, Cmnd. 827, August 1959.

National Board for Prices and Incomes, Report No. 34, *Bank Charges*, Cmnd. 3292, May 1967.

Committee to Review the Functioning of Financial Institutions, *Report*, Cmnd. 7937, June 1980.

Newspapers and Magazines

The Economist.
Times.

Secondary Sources

Books and Articles

Aikman, David, Oliver Bush, and Alan M. Taylor. "Monetary Versus Macroprudential Policies: Causal Impacts of Interest Rates and Credit Controls in the Era of the Radcliffe Report, Working Paper 22380." *NBER Working Paper Series*, National Bureau of Economic Research, June 2016. 1–43.

Akerlof, George A., and Robert Shiller, J. *Animal Spirits: How Human Psychology Drives the Economy and Why It Matters for Global Capitalism.* 9th ed. Princeton: Princeton University Press, 2009. Reprint, 2010.

Allen, William A. *Monetary Policy and Financial Repression in Britain, 1951–59.* Basingstoke: Palgrave Macmillan, 2014.

Anginer, Deniz, Asli Demirgüç-Kunt, and Min Zhu. "How Does Bank Competition Affect Systemic Stability? World Bank Policy Working Paper Number 5981." *World Bank Policy Research Working Papers*, The World Bank, February 2012. 1–39.

Artis, M. J. "Monetary Policy Part II." In *British Economic Policy 1960–74*, edited by F. T. Blackaby, 258–303. Cambridge: Cambridge University Press, 1978.

Barth, James R., Gerard Caprio Jr., and Ross Levine. "Bank Regulation and Supervision in 180 Countries from 1999 to 2011, Working Paper 18733." *NBER Working Paper Series*, National Bureau of Economic Research, January 2013. 1–110.

Bátiz-Lazo, Bernardo. "Emergence and Evolution of ATM Networks in the UK, 1967–2000." *Business History* 51, no. 1 (2009): 1–27.

Beck, Thorsten, Asli Demirgüç-Kunt, and Ross Levine. "Bank Concentration and Crises, Working Paper 9921." *NBER Working Paper Series*, National Bureau of Economic Research, 2003. 1–41.

Beck, Thorsten, Asli Demirgüç-Kunt, and Ross Levine. "Bank Concentration, Competition, and Crises: First Results." *Journal of Banking & Finance* 30, (2006). Accessed 30 March 2017. http://www.sciencedirect.com.

Beck, Thorsten, Olivier De Jonghe, and Glenn Schepens. "Bank Competition and Stability: Cross-Country Heterogeneity." *Journal of Financial Intermediation* 22, no. 2 (2013): 218–44. Accessed 24 March 2017. http://dx.doi.org/10.1016/j.jfi.2012.07.001.

Berger, Allen N., Leora F. Klapper, and Rima Turk-Ariss. "Bank Competition and Financial Stability, World Bank Policy Research Working Paper 4696." *World Bank Policy Research Working Papers*, The World Bank, August 2008. 1–32.

Boyd, John H., Gianni De Nicolò, and Abu M. Jalal. "Bank Risk-Taking and Competition Revisited: New Theory and New Evidence, WP/06/297." *IMF Working Papers*, December 2006. 1–49.

Capie, Forrest, and Mark Billings. "Profitability in English Banking in the Twentieth Century." *European Review of Economic History* 5, no. 3 (2001): 367–401.

Claessens, Stijn, and Luc Laeven. "What Drives Bank Competition? Some International Evidence." *Journal of Money, Credit and Banking* 36, no. 3, Part 2 (2003): 563–83.

Claessens, Stijn, and M. Ayhan Kose. "Financial Crises: Explanations, Types, and Implications, WP/13/28." *IMF Working Papers*, International Monetary Fund, January 2013. 1–65.

de-Ramon, Sebastian J. A., and Michael Straughan. "Measuring Competition in the UK Deposit-Taking Sector, Staff Working Paper No. 631." *Staff Working Papers*, Bank of England, December 2016. 1–42.

Fear, Jeffrey. "Cartels." In *The Oxford Handbook of Business History*, edited by Geoffrey G. Jones and Jonathan Zeitlin, 1–18. Oxford: Oxford University Press, September 2009. Accessed 26 October 2014. http://www.oxford-handbooks.com.

Goodhart, Charles A. E. "Competition and Credit Control: Some Personal Reflections." *Financial History Review* 22, no. 2 (2015): 235–46.

Gorton, Gary B. "The Quiet Period and Its End." In *Misunderstanding Financial Crises: Why We Don't See Them Coming*, 125–33. New York, NY: Oxford University Press, 2012.

Griffiths, Brian. *Competition in Banking*. London: Institute of Economic Affairs, 1970.

Heffernan, Sheila. *Modern Banking*. Chichester: Wiley, 2009.

Holmes, A. R., and Edwin Green. *Midland: 150 Years of Banking Business.* London: BT Batsford Ltd., 1986.

Keeley, Michael C. "Deposit Insurance, Risk, and Market Power in Banking." *The American Economic Review* 80, no. 5 (December 1990): 1183–1200.

Kynaston, David. *Austerity Britain: 1945–1951.* London: Bloomsbury Publishing plc, 2008.

Laeven, Luc, Lev Ratnovski, and Hui Tong. "Bank Size and Systemic Risk, SDN/14/04." *IMF Staff Discussion Notes*, International Monetary Fund, May 2014. 1–33.

MacLeod, Rory. "The Promise of Full Employment." In *War and Social Change: British Society in the Second World War*, edited by Harold L. Smith. Manchester: Manchester University Press, 1986.

Merton, Robert K. "The Unanticipated Consequences of Purposive Social Action." *American Sociological Review* 1, no. 6 (December 1936): 894–904.

Michie, Ranald C. "Suppression, Regulation, and Evasion: 1939–70." In *The Global Securities Market: A History*, 205–52. Oxford: Oxford University Press, 2006.

Newton, Lucy. "Government, the Banks and Industry in Inter-War Britain." In *Business and Politics in Europe, 1900–1970*, edited by Terry Gourvish, 145–68. Cambridge: Cambridge University Press, 2003.

The Organisation for Economic Co-operation and Development. *Bank Competition and Financial Stability.* OECD Publishing, 2011. Accessed 1 August 2018. http://www.oecd.org/daf/fin/financial-markets/48501035.pdf.

Reid, Margaret. "The Dash for Growth—And Its Consequences." In *The Secondary Banking Crisis, 1973–75: Its Causes and Course*, 70–85. London: Macmillan, 1982.

Reid, Margaret. *Secondary Banking Crisis, 1973–75: Its Causes and Course.* London: Macmillan, 1982.

Revell, J. R. S. *Costs and Margins in Banking: An International Survey.* Edited by Organisation for Economic Co-operation and Development. Paris: Organisation for Economic Co-operation and Development, 1980.

Sampson, Anthony. *Anatomy of Britain.* London: Hodder and Stoughton, 1962.

Schenk, Catherine. "Rogue Trading at Lloyds Bank International, 1974: Operational Risk in Volatile Markets." *Business History Review* 91, no. 1 (2017): 105–28.

Schenk, Catherine R. "Britain in the World Economy." In *A Companion to Contemporary Britain, 1939–2000*, edited by Paul Addison and Harriet Jones, 463–81. Oxford: Blackwell, 2007.

Schooner, Heidi Mandanis, and Michael Taylor. "Convergence and Competition: The Case of Bank Regulation in Britain and the United States." *Michigan Journal of International Law* 20, no. 4 (Summer 1999): 595–656.

Tew, J. H. B. "Monetary Policy Part I." In *British Economic Policy 1960–74*, edited by F. T. Blackaby, 218–57. Cambridge: Cambridge University Press, 1978.

Tomlinson, Jim. "Economic Policy." In *The Cambridge Economic History of Modern Britain Volume 3: Structural Change and Growth, 1939–2000*, edited by Roderick Floud and Paul Johnson, 189–212. Cambridge: Cambridge University Press, 2008.

Vives, Xavier. "Competition and Stability in Banking, WP-852." *Working Papers*, IESE Business School, University of Navarra, April 2010. 2–55.

Watson, Katherine. "The Financial Services Sector Since 1945." In *The Cambridge Economic History of Modern Britain Volume 3: Structural Change and Growth, 1939–2000*, edited by Roderick Floud and Paul Johnson, 167–88. Cambridge: Cambridge University Press, March 2008. Accessed 19 September 2017. http://www.cambridge.org/core.

Wilks, Stephen. *In the Public Interest: Competition Policy and the Monopolies and Mergers Commission*. Manchester: Manchester University Press, 1999.

CHAPTER 4

Bank Regulation Today

Abstract Having reviewed the approach to bank regulation taken in the period from 1946 to the early 1970s, this chapter reflects upon the nature of bank regulation and supervision since the global financial crisis. The response to the crisis has tended to be technocratic, reflecting a preference—which began to emerge in the 1970s—for codified, detailed and often highly technical rules, evident, for example, in the revised requirements for bank capital. These rules have emanated from national legislation, EU directives and regulations, and Basel III, and have been accompanied by the further development of complex regulatory and supervisory structures. This raises the question as to whether the very strong focus on codified rules has been at the expense of regulation in other forms.

Keywords Basel III · Capital Requirements Directive IV package · Legitimacy · Codified regulation · Global financial crisis · Deposit insurance

In this penultimate chapter, some observations are made about the nature of bank regulation since the global financial crisis in the context of the review of post-war bank regulation in Chapters 2 and 3. Following a financial or banking crisis, there is often—understandably—a strong regulatory reaction and the response to the global financial crisis 2007–2009 has been no exception, in both its scale and scope. Of relevance

© The Author(s) 2018

L. Arch, *The Regulation of the London Clearing Banks, 1946–1971*, Palgrave Studies in Economic History,
https://doi.org/10.1007/978-3-030-00910-6_4

to UK banks has been regulation emanating from the UK government, the EU, the Basel Committee on Banking Supervision, and the Group of Twenty (the "G20").

The regulatory response has unfolded in two overlapping phases. First, there were measures intended to contain and manage and the immediate crisis and to deal with failing banks and financial institutions. The Banking (Special Provisions) Act 2008 enabled authorized UK deposit-takers to be taken into public ownership in certain circumstances, and this power was used in relation to Northern Rock plc.[1] The Banking Act 2009 established a special resolution regime for dealing with failing banks together with a new bank insolvency procedure.[2] Beyond the management and containment of the crisis phase of the response were those measures designed to restore, maintain and strengthen the stability of financial and banking systems. These have included micro-prudential measures (focused on controlling the behaviour of individual units within the system through supervision) and macro-prudential ones, addressing the stability of the banking system as a whole. They have often involved the development of supranational, international and/or national regulatory and supervisory structures. In the UK, the Financial Services Act 2012, effective from 1 April 2013, abolished the Financial Services Authority and replaced it with the Financial Conduct Authority (FCA) and Prudential Regulation Authority. The Financial Services (Banking Reform) Act 2013 introduced, among other things, the "ring-fencing" of retail and SME deposit-taking activities by banks from other activities. The development of effective supranational, international regulatory and supervisory structures is not straightforward, however. As Schenk has observed, "regulation and supervision of the banking sector are so central to a state's economy that governments are very reluctant to delegate these powers."[3]

A number of new EU directives and regulations have been adopted since the crisis, including the Capital Requirements Directive (CRD) IV "package" to implement Basel III. This package consists of Directive 2013/36/EU (referred to as the Capital Requirements Directive) and Regulation (EU) No 575/2013 on prudential requirements for credit institutions and investment firms. Directive 2014/59/EU (referred to as the Bank Recovery and Resolution Directive) was introduced with effect from January 2016. In parallel with implementing these regulations and directives the EU is also seeking to "complete" the Banking Union. Two of its three pillars are in place, namely the Single Supervisory Mechanism (the first pillar) and the Single Resolution Mechanism (the second) to resolve banks. The establishment of the third pillar of the Banking Union, a European Deposit Insurance Scheme, is not yet complete. A European Systemic Risk Board (ESRB) has also been established with a macro-prudential role. It monitors and assesses potential threats to financial stability that arise from macroeconomic developments and from developments within the financial system as a whole. This focus on macro-prudential regulation has been another hallmark of regulation since the crisis.

In addition to UK government legislation and EU legislation, a regulatory framework for internationally active banks—the Basel III framework—has emerged under the aegis of the Basel Committee on Banking Supervision.[4] Basel III has focused on the quality and level of bank capital (in its Pillars 1, 2 and 3) and on standards of bank liquidity (through a Liquidity Coverage Ratio and a Net Stable Funding Ratio).[5] The very largest global banks—global systemically important banks or "G-SIBS"—are subject to additional regulatory requirements. Finally, the Financial Stability Board established by the Group of Twenty in 2009 as a successor to the Financial Stability Forum has a mandate to coordinate at an international level the work of national financial authorities and international standard setting bodies.

It can be seen from the above brief survey that since the global financial crisis, the trend towards a style of regulation which is formal and codified, and focused on structures—evident since the 1970s—has continued, as has the preference for detailed rules. These rules have tended towards greater complexity reflecting the more complex nature of banks and the often global nature of their operations.[6] To give one example, Basel III requires adherence to a Liquidity Coverage Ratio "to promote the short-term resilience of the liquidity risk profile of banks."[7] This one ratio alone takes 75 pages to explicate. Although it is not an exact equivalent, the liquidity ratio as used by the London clearing banks in the period up until 1971, can be defined in a few words—see Fig. 2.3 in Chapter 2. The more codified regulatory framework for banks which has emerged since the 1970s may be explained by Vogel's hypothesis that freer markets require more rules, not fewer. He thus argues that the period since around 1975 has not been a period of deregulation, as many assume, but a period of liberalization coupled with various forms of reregulation. This reregulatory trend, he argues, has tended to be "juridical" in nature, with informal rules being replaced with legal ones and tacit rules with codified ones.[8] The emergence of a liberalized but highly regulated environment for the City of London since the 1970 and 1980s fits well with Vogel's hypothesis.

As mentioned earlier, great emphasis has been placed since the crisis on increasing the quality and level of bank capital. For example, six of the sixteen core indicators of financial soundness used by the IMF are concerned with bank capital reflecting its importance in contemporary regulation.[9] Capital adequacy has also featured prominently in the EU's approach to bank regulation since the crisis, as reflected in the CRD IV package. Under Basel III, total capital must be at least 8% of risk-weighted assets at all times. Common Equity, Tier 1 (which includes common shares and retained earnings) must be at least 4.5% of risk-weighted assets at all times.[10] Admati and Hellwig have argued that increasing the ratio of bank equity to bank borrowing is the key to a more stable banking system.[11] This is the logical corollary to their contention that "significantly reducing the reliance of large banks on borrowing is the most straightforward and cost-effective approach to crisis prevention."[12] However, this elides the fact that the liabilities side of a bank's balance sheet is intrinsically different from that of a non-bank. The former includes not only borrowings in the conventional sense of the term, but also customer deposits. As receiving deposits is a core function of a retail bank, its balance sheet structure is inherently different from that of other firms, and as long as this remains a core function, bank balance sheets will tend to have a high ratio of borrowings to equity. Nevertheless, Admati and Hellwig suggest that "much" higher levels of bank capital are needed than are required under Basel III.[13] Navajas and Thegeya, based on their research into the Financial Soundness Indicators (FSIs) for 80 countries over the period 2005–2012, identified that two of the soundness indicators, regulatory capital to risk-weighted assets and return on equity, were negatively and contemporaneously strongly correlated with the occurrence of banking crises. This research thus lends support to the regulatory emphasis on the quantity and quality of bank capital. Their period of analysis is, however, rather short given that, as they themselves note, "consistent" reporting of FSIs only begins after 2008. In addition, the period 2008–2012 would have been rather less typical than other periods, having been dominated by the global financial crisis.[14] Schaeck and Čihák found that competition in banking may itself encourage banks to hold more capital. Their research was based upon 8584 bank-year observations for ten European countries during the period 1999–2004 with the Panzar and Rosse H-statistic used to measure competition. It concluded that competition can render banks more prudent.[15]

On the other hand, other recent research has questioned the regulatory emphasis on bank capital. Jordà et al. make the point that there has been a very long-term decline in bank capital. In 1870, bank capital ratios commonly exceeded 30%. In many countries, capital ratios decreased between 1870 and 1945. They were then relatively stable at under 10% in the decades after the Second World War and have settled at between 5 and 10% in recent decades.[16] They contend that higher capital ratios are unlikely to prevent systemic financial crises and that higher capitals ratio are not a good predictor of a system's resilience to financial crises. However, higher capital may mitigate the social and economic costs of crises if they do occur (and may therefore be justifiable) because countries with well-capitalized banks tend to recover from crises more quickly.[17] Kobrak and Troege argue that the focus on capital adequacy since Basel I has been misguided. Beginning in 1988, the development and implementation of the Basel Capital Accord involved regulators "placing a bet on a methodology that has not produced a reliable framework for prudential regulation and perhaps even blocked other approaches."[18] This was because the "complex bargaining process" in which the banks and regulators engaged was focused on the need to reduce "the cost of future bailouts rather than to stabilize the banking sector."[19] The focus on capital adequacy also sits uneasily with evidence from the post-war period in the UK. Billings and Capie analyzed published capital as a percentage of total assets for UK banks and found that it reached "historically low levels during the 1950s," standing at a mere 2.8% from 1950 to 1959.[20] This low level of bank capital does however need to be seen in the context of strict control over the issue of new capital by the Capital Issues Committee up until the late 1950s. Even had banks wished to increase their capital by issuing new capital this may not have been possible. It should be noted that from 1959, once the restrictions on issuing new capital began to be relaxed, bank capital did increase.

A common feature of regulatory structures today—and pillar three of the EU's Banking Union—is deposit protection. The Banking Act 1979 introduced a mandatory Deposit Protection Fund for the first time, for deposits with licensed deposit-takers and recognized banks in the UK, protecting 75% of the first £10,000 of deposits.[21] It was funded by the recognized banks and licensed deposit-takers themselves. The intention behind the fund was to reduce the risk of a run on a bank.

Deposit protection, it is argued, creates moral hazard. This may distort the incentives of both banks and depositors, which in turn may cause or exacerbate systemic risk. Banks may be inclined to take on greater risk when deposit protection is in place because, if their bank fails, depositors would be protected from loss. Deposit protection may thus provide a structural incentive for banks to take greater risks. Moreover, deposit protection may mean that individual depositors do not have an incentive to monitor their bank. This argument has some support in the literature. Demirgüç-Kunt and Detragiache, based on the research into deposit insurance systems during the period 1980–1997 in 61 countries, found that "explicit deposit insurance tends to be detrimental to bank stability."[22] In a similar vein, using survey data about bank regulatory and supervisory practices in 107 countries, Barth, Caprio Jr. and Levine sought to examine the impact of those practices on the development, efficiency and fragility of the banking sector. They also found that "generous deposit insurance schemes are strongly and negatively associated with bank stability."[23] Beck, De Jonghe and Schepens found that the impact of competition on stability is amplified if there are strict activity restrictions on banks or generous deposit insurance.[24] Calomiris and Haber assert that in the absence of deposit protection "depositors can [...] discipline bank insiders by withdrawing their funds when the insiders take imprudent risks."[25] Arguably, it is almost impossible in practice for individual depositors to make such judgements. Lloyds Banking Group's *Annual Report and Accounts 2017* runs to 276 pages and it would be difficult for a layperson to evaluate whether the bank was taking "imprudent risks," based on the financial statements presented in that document.[26] The absence of deposit protection until 1979 meant this type of moral hazard was avoided. It should be noted on the other hand that there was a run on Northern Rock plc in September 2007, despite the existence of deposit protection. Prior to then, there had not been a run on a significant UK bank since the run on Overend Gurney & Co. in 1866.[27]

The regulatory response to the global financial crisis—with its focus on the development and implementation of codified and detailed rules and the establishment, or further development, of elaborate regulatory and supervisory structures at national, international and supranational levels has been a technocratic one. While this may have been inevitable given the complexity of banks, banking systems and bank regulation, it is important to consider in addition how to strengthen that other dimension of the regulatory framework—the set of informal institutions which regulate conduct. As Searle points out:

> The essential role of human institutions and the purpose of having institutions is not to constrain people as such, but, rather, to create new sorts of power relationships. Human institutions are, above all, *enabling*, because they create power, but it is a special kind of power. It is the power that is marked by such terms as: rights, duties, obligations, authorizations, permissions, empowerments, requirements, and certifications. I call all of these *deontic powers*.[28]

It is not obvious how the regulator's deontic powers have been strengthened as part of the regulatory response to the crisis. While the laws, directives and regulations enacted since the crisis have created a very strong material incentive to comply with regulation through the threat of punishment, what has been done to enhance the legitimacy of the regulator by strengthening its deontic powers? If a regulator is highly legitimate, its regulations will be considered binding by those it regulates. As Tyler has argued, "legitimacy has an influence upon behaviour that is equal to or greater than that of the risk of punishment."[29] The legitimacy of the regulator could thus be considered at the heart of effective regulation.

Notes

1. Banking (Special Provisions) Act 2008, *legislation.gov.uk*, accessed 21 June 2018, http://www.legislation.gov.uk/ukpga/2008/2/contents.
2. Banking Act 2009, *legislation.gov.uk*, accessed 21 June 2018, http://www.legislation.gov.uk/ukpga/2009/1/pdfs/ukpga_20090001_en.pdf.
3. Catherine Schenk, "Bank Regulation and Supervision," in *The Oxford Handbook of Banking and Financial History*, ed. Youssef Cassis, Catherine Schenk, and Richard Grossman, Oxford Handbooks (Oxford: Oxford University Press, July 2016): Conclusions.
4. The Basel Committee on Banking Supervision, "Basel III: A Global Regulatory Framework for More Resilient Banks and Banking Systems" (Bank for International Settlements, December 2010, revised June 2011), accessed 31 July 2018, http://www.bis.org/publ/bcbs189.pdf.
5. "Basel Committee on Banking Supervision Reforms—Basel III," *Bank for International Settlements*, accessed 21 June 2018, https://www.bis.org/bcbs/basel3/b3_bank_sup_reforms.pdf.

6. This is not exclusively the case. There are examples of principles-based, rather than rules-based, approaches to bank supervision and regulation prevailing since the global financial crisis. For example, the Basel Committee on Banking Supervision reviewed and re-issued its "Core *Principles* [my emphasis] for Effective Banking Supervision," in September 2012. See "Core Principles for Effective Banking Supervision," *Bank for International Settlements*, accessed 22 June 2018, https://www.bis.org/publ/bcbs230.htm.
7. The Basel Committee on Banking Supervision, "Basel III: The Liquidity Coverage Ratio and Liquidity Risk Monitoring Tools" (Bank for International Settlements, January 2013): para. 14, accessed 20 August 2018, http://www.bis.org/publ/bcbs238.pdf.
8. Steven K. Vogel, *Freer Markets, More Rules: Regulatory Reform in Advanced Industrial Countries* (Ithaca, NY: Cornell University Press, 1998): 16–17.
9. These are indicators I01, I02, I03, I04, I05 and I16. "Financial Soundness Indicators and the IMF," *International Monetary Fund*, accessed 22 August 2017, https://www.imf.org/external/np/sta/fsi/eng/fsi.htm, Table 2. The original indicators were revised in November 2013.
10. Basel Committee on Banking Supervision, "Basel III: A Global Regulatory Framework for More Resilient Banks and Banking Systems," Annex 1.
11. Anat Admati and Martin Hellwig, *The Bankers' New Clothes: What's Wrong with Banking and What to Do About It* (Princeton, NJ: Princeton University Press, 2013): 79–166.
12. Ibid., 13.
13. Ibid., 178.
14. Matias Costa Navajas and Aaron Thegeya, "Financial Soundness Indicators and Banking Crises," in *IMF Working Papers* (IMF, 2013): 3, 18–19.
15. Klaus Schaeck and Martin Čihák, "Banking Competition and Capital Ratios, WP/07/216," in *IMF Working Papers* (International Monetary Fund, September 2007): 21–22.
16. Òscar Jordà et al., "Bank Capital Redux: Solvency, Liquidity, and Crisis, Working Paper 23287," in *NBER Working Paper Series* (Cambridge, MA: National Bureau of Economic Research, March 2017): 6–7.
17. Ibid., 34.
18. Christopher Kobrak and Michael Troege, "From Basel to Bailouts: Forty Years of International Attempts to Bolster Bank Safety," *Financial History Review* 22, no. 2 (2015): 148. The first accord was published in July 1988, see "International Convergence of Capital Measurement and Capital Standards," *Bank for International Settlements*, accessed 24 August 2018, http://www.bis.org/publ/bcbs04a.htm.

19. Ibid., 142.
20. Mark Billings and Forrest Capie, "Capital in British Banking, 1920–1970," *Business History* 49, no. 2 (March 2007): 144. Jordà et al. give the lowest capital ratio between 1870 and 2008 for the UK as being in 1982 at 4.1%. Jordà et al., "Bank Capital Redux: Solvency, Liquidity, and Crisis, Working Paper 23287," Table 3. Billings and Capie's figure of 2.8% is, however, based on published capital which was lower than "true" capital.
21. The deposit compensation limit in the UK is £85,000 per person per firm (for claims against firms declared in default from 30 January 2017), see *Financial Services Compensation Board*, accessed 24 August 2018, https://www.fscs.org.uk/what-we-cover/compensation-limits/. This derives from EU Directive 2014/49/EU.
22. Asli Demirgüç-Kunt and Enrica Detragiache, "Does Deposit Insurance Increase Banking System Stability? An Empirical Investigation," *Journal of Monetary Economics* 49 (2002): 1402.
23. James R. Barth, Gerard Caprio Jr., and Ross Levine, "Bank Regulation and Supervision: What Works Best?" *Journal of Financial Intermediation* 13 (2004): 245. They also argue that restricting the activities of banks, and greater supervisory oversight, are not associated with stability.
24. Thorsten Beck, Olivier De Jonghe, and Glenn Schepens, "Bank Competition and Stability: Cross-Country Heterogeneity," *Journal of Financial Intermediation* 22, no. 2 (2013): 240, accessed 24 March 2017, http://dx.doi.org/10.1016/j.jfi.2012.07.001.
25. Charles W. Calomiris and Stephen H. Haber, *Fragile by Design: The Political Origins of Banking Crises and Scarce Credit* (Princeton, NJ: Princeton University Press, 2014; reprint, 2016): 37.
26. "Lloyds Banking Group Annual Report and Accounts 2017," accessed 22 June 2018, http://www.lloydsbankinggroup.com/globalassets/documents/investors/2017/2017_lbg_annual_report_v3.pdf.
27. For an account of events leading to the run on deposits, see "The Demise of Overend Gurney," *Bank of England Quarterly Bulletin* (Quarter 2, 2016): 98–99, accessed 12 July 2018, https://www.bankofengland.co.uk/quarterly-bulletin/2016/q2/the-demise-of-overend-gurney. The City of Glasgow Bank did not experience a conventional bank run involving depositors at the time of its failure in 1878, but a 'silent' one in the wholesale markets.
28. John R. Searle, "What Is an Institution?" *Journal of Institutional Economics* 1, no. 1 (2005): 10.
29. Tom R. Tyler, "Legitimacy and Criminal Justice: The Benefits of Self-Regulation," *Ohio State Journal of Criminal Law* 7 (2009): 318.

References

Secondary Sources

Books and Articles

Admati, Anat, and Martin Hellwig. *The Bankers' New Clothes: What's Wrong with Banking and What to Do About It*. Princeton, NJ: Princeton University Press, 2013.

Barth, James R., Gerard Caprio Jr., and Ross Levine. "Bank Regulation and Supervision: What Works Best?" *Journal of Financial Intermediation* 13, (2004): 205–48.

The Basel Committee on Banking Supervision. *Basel III: A Global Regulatory Framework for More Resilient Banks and Banking Systems*. Bank for International Settlements, December 2010, revised June 2011. Accessed 31 July 2018. http://www.bis.org/publ/bcbs189.pdf.

The Basel Committee on Banking Supervision. *Basel III: The Liquidity Coverage Ratio and Liquidity Risk Monitoring Tools*. Bank for International Settlements, January 2013. Accessed 20 August 2018. http://www.bis.org/publ/bcbs238.pdf.

Beck, Thorsten, Olivier De Jonghe, and Glenn Schepens. "Bank Competition and Stability: Cross-Country Heterogeneity." *Journal of Financial Intermediation* 22, no. 2 (2013): 218–44. Accessed 24 March 2017. http://dx.doi.org/10.1016/j.jfi.2012.07.001.

Billings, Mark, and Forrest Capie. "Capital in British Banking, 1920–1970." *Business History* 49, no. 2 (March 2007): 139–62.

Calomiris, Charles W., and Stephen H. Haber. *Fragile by Design: The Political Origins of Banking Crises and Scarce Credit*. Princeton, NJ: Princeton University Press, 2014. Reprint, 2016.

Demirgüç-Kunt, Asli, and Enrica Detragiache. "Does Deposit Insurance Increase Banking System Stability? An Empirical Investigation." *Journal of Monetary Economics* 49, (2002): 1373–1406.

Jordà, Òscar, Björn Richter, Moritz Schularick, and Alan M. Taylor. "Bank Capital Redux: Solvency, Liquidity, and Crisis, Working Paper 23287." *NBER Working Paper Series*, National Bureau of Economic Research, March 2017. 1–37.

Kobrak, Christopher, and Michael Troege. "From Basel to Bailouts: Forty Years of International Attempts to Bolster Bank Safety." *Financial History Review* 22, no. 2 (2015): 133–56.

Navajas, Matias Costa, and Aaron Thegeya. "Financial Soundness Indicators and Banking Crises." *IMF Working Papers*, IMF, 2013. 1–38.

Schaeck, Klaus, and Martin Čihák. "Banking Competition and Capital Ratios, WP/07/216." *IMF Working Papers*, International Monetary Fund, September 2007. 1–40.

Schenk, Catherine. "Bank Regulation and Supervision." In *The Oxford Handbook of Banking and Financial History*, edited by Youssef Cassis, Catherine Schenk, and Richard Grossman. Oxford: Oxford University Press, July 2016. Accessed 6 January 2017. http://www.oxfordhandbooks.com/view/10.1093/oxfordhb/9780199658626.001.0001/oxfordhb-9780199658626-e-19.

Searle, John R. "What Is an Institution?" *Journal of Institutional Economics* 1, no. 1 (2005): 1–22.

Tyler, Tom R. "Legitimacy and Criminal Justice: The Benefits of Self-Regulation." *Ohio State Journal of Criminal Law* 7 (2009): 307–59.

Vogel, Steven K. *Freer Markets, More Rules: Regulatory Reform in Advanced Industrial Countries*. Ithaca, NY: Cornell University Press, 1998.

CHAPTER 5

Conclusion

Abstract This chapter returns to the economic and industry context. It comments on the way in which the structure of the banking and financial services industry had changed by the end of the 1970s, and on the relationship between the changed structure of the industry and broader structural and ideational changes. It reflects upon the implications of these changes for bank regulation. Finally, it highlights two issues which need to be at heart of thinking about bank regulation in the coming years.

Keywords Trust in banking · Trustworthy banks · Monetarism · Informal regulation

As was seen in Chapter 3, the banking and financial services industry grew continuously over the period from 1946. The rate of growth in the sector accelerated during the 1970s and beyond. The 1970s in particular could be considered a period of explosive growth. Over the longer period from 1955 until 2000, there was a marked—but by no means precipitous—decline in the assets of the banking sector as a percentage of assets of all UK financial institutions, from 55.6% of to 39.7%.

Within banking specifically, a number of structural changes were underway. First, although banking and financial services was an industry of functional specialisms—there were several distinct types of banks,

© The Author(s) 2018

L. Arch, *The Regulation of the London Clearing Banks, 1946–1971*, Palgrave Studies in Economic History,
https://doi.org/10.1007/978-3-030-00910-6_5

including the clearing banks, the merchant banks, savings banks, the British overseas banks and foreign banks—the distinctions between types of bank were becoming blurred. For example, the giro account offered by the National Girobank (which had been established in 1968 out of the Post Office Savings Bank) was a non-interest-bearing current account similar to the current account offered by the London clearing banks. In 1970, the National Girobank began to offer personal loans for the first time via the Mercantile Credit Company Ltd. The regulatory framework mirrored and reinforced this trend. For example, the new reserve ratio under CCC in 1971 applied to the entire banking system reflecting the view that from a regulatory perspective, the banking system should be regarded not as a system of different types of bank, each with their own specialism, but as homogeneous. Accordingly, the clearing banks, merchant banks, foreign banks in London, finance houses (albeit with transitional arrangements) and certain bank subsidiaries were all covered by the new reserve ratio requirement, although the savings banks, the National Girobank and the building societies were outside its scope.

In addition to the slow dissolution of functional specialisms, a second trend was the growth in the overseas banks, particularly American banks. The overseas banks competed with the clearing banks as takers of deposits and as lenders but tended to operate in the wholesale rather than the retail market. The 1960s in particular saw a "headlong rush of US banks into London."[1] The arrival of overseas banks in the 1960s had been facilitated by the Bank's liberal approach to overseas banks establishing themselves in the City, while the establishment by American banks of branches in London had been given impetus by changes in the regulatory framework for banks in the US. As at 28 February 1959, "Overseas and Foreign Banks" held current and deposit accounts in the UK of £922 million (and made advances of £279 million), a fraction of the amount held by the clearing banks.[2] By the end of 1970, however, deposits with American banks in the UK alone exceeded the amount held by the clearing banks.[3] In the four-year period from 1966 to 1970, the number of foreign banks grew from 103 to 159.[4] More generally, the importance of the non-clearing banks (including the foreign banks) grew. Between 1970 and 1975, deposits held by non-clearing banks increased from £1452 million to £21,590 million.[5]

A third important structural change in banking was the growth in non-sterling assets and liabilities held by the sector, including by the clearing banks. By 1975, UK banking sector assets amounted to

£139,700 million of which £84,839 million were loans and advances in currencies other than sterling, while £85,152 of its liabilities were deposits in currencies other than sterling. Thus, by the mid-1970s, 61% of the balance sheet of the UK banking sector took the form of non-sterling assets and liabilities.[6]

By the mid-1970s, banks were still the dominant type of financial institution although the pre-eminence of the London clearing banks within that sector, measured by assets, had disappeared. How should this change be interpreted? Did their declining share of the banking market indicate that the London clearing banks were uncompetitive? Chapter 3 considered the evidence concerning the degree of concentration and competition in clearing banking in the period. It was seen that clearing banking was moderately concentrated and that although there was limited price competition—certain clearing bank prices were uniform, having been set collectively by the CLCB—there were other indicators of competition in clearing banking. From the perspective of competition policy, for example, there was not a monopoly in clearing banking and there were no mergers between the Big Five banks until 1968. On the other hand, certain restrictive trade practices (such as uniform branch opening hours) prevailed. The NBPI report in 1967 into bank charges—a key indicator of the degree of competition—concluded that the prices charged by the clearing banks were reasonable, even though some of these were set collectively by the cartel. There is also evidence that the clearing banks were open to change and did innovate. These dispositions are more likely to be present in an industry which is competitive than in one which is not competitive. A considerable body of empirical research indicates that competition in banking tends to make banking systems more stable. If this is correct, the high degree of stability may have been an indicator of the presence of a reasonable degree of competition.

How did the changing structure of the industry and interact with broader changes? In both the UK and internationally, there were structural and ideational shifts from the late 1960s and early 1970s which heralded the emergence of a more liberalized and more globalized international economic order. Chapter 3 began by considering some the key economic and market trends in the UK during the period 1946 until the late 1970s (see Figs. 3.1–3.10 in Chapter 3). It was seen that from the late 1960s a number of key macroeconomic variables were either deteriorating or becoming more volatile. For example, the rate of inflation, which had been increasing gradually from its postwar low in 1959, had by now begun to increase much more rapidly. Between 1967 and 1971 the annual rate of inflation would increase from 2.5 to 9.4%. As well as changes in the structure of the UK economy, there were changes in the international economic order such as the move to floating rather than fixed-but-adjustable exchange rates in the early 1970s. In addition, there were profound ideational changes, particularly in economic thinking (reflected in the greater influence of monetarism and the view that the control of inflation was the prime objective of economic policy). These changes coincided with the disintegration of the postwar regulatory framework for banking and the move away from the policy of financial repression.

These structural and ideational shifts had implications for bank regulation and shifted its focal point. The London clearing banks became less pivotal to the operation of the regulatory framework. Until 1972, governments had attempted to balance the balance of payments on current account by working through the clearing banking system. It is worth re-iterating quite how different this aspect of the economic context was compared with that which pertains today when currency exchange rates are determined by the market. Before 1972, the balance on the current account influenced the nature and timing of regulatory interventions in the banking system because the authorities responded to imbalances in the balance of payments on current transactions by restricting domestic credit, operating through the clearing banks. After the move to a floating exchange rate in June 1972, restricting the availability of credit through direct controls over bank lending was no longer central to the execution of regulatory and monetary policy in quite the same way.

The growing influence of monetarism and the establishment of the control of inflation as the primary objective of monetary policy also led to a change in regulatory focus.[7] Monetarism represented a new and different understanding of the role and importance of the instruments, indicators and goals of monetary policy.[8] Needham sees the radical regulatory change in 1971—CCC—as the outcome, among other things, of the intellectual conversion of key Bank and Treasury officials to monetarism.[9] The origin of this conversion, he argues, can be traced to 1967 and 1968 when monetarist ideas began to influence thinking in the Bank and Treasury through their discussions with the IMF. There was intensive contact with the IMF in 1967 necessitated by the negotiation of a $1.4 billion loan approved in November of that year. Then, in October 1968, the UK hosted a week-long seminar on Domestic Credit Expansion (DCE) involving Bank officials, Treasury officials and representatives of the IMF. DCE was an indicator of growth in the money supply adjusted for the external account. The October seminar was the "catalyst" for a fundamental review of monetary policy. At around the same time, a Money Supply Group was formed within the Bank. In February 1970, the Money Supply Group submitted its interim report to a Treasury Group on Monetary Policy (TGMP) and this was followed by the publication of a research paper, "The Importance of Money" in the *Bank of England Quarterly Bulletin* in June 1970.[10] In March 1971 the TGMP, informed by the work of the Money Supply Group, published its final report. Officials in the Bank and Treasury were well-advanced on their journey towards monetarism.

A core tenet of monetarism was that the stock of money was a key indicator (or intermediate target) of monetary policy. Controlling the money supply was in turn the key to controlling inflation, the goal of monetary policy. Officials were becoming convinced both that there was a predictable relationship between the demand-for-money in the economy and GDP output which could be expressed econometrically, and that the velocity of circulation of money was stable, or at least more stable than had been assumed previously. The key instrument for controlling the stock of money was the rate of interest and once CCC was introduced, the bank rate changed much more frequently. While CCC did not include an explicit target for the growth of the money supply, over the period from 1969 to 1979 money supply growth targets became established (and an early form of a money supply growth target took the form of a DCE ceiling of £400 million, agreed in May 1969). In March 1971, Barber's budget set out that the money supply needed to grow by not less than around 3% per quarter.

The changed understanding of the role and importance of monetary policy reflected in CCC would change the relationship between the state and the Bank of England, and between the state and the clearing banks. In terms of the latter, before CCC in September 1971 the clearing banks were the principal agents upon or through which monetary policy instruments worked. This reinforced their status relative to other banks who did not play the same role. Instruments such as the cash and liquidity ratios, Special Deposits, and quantitative and qualitative guidance worked primarily (though not exclusively in the case of quantitative and qualitative guidance) through the clearing banks. After CCC, instruments such as the reserve asset ratio, Special Deposits, Supplementary Special Deposits, and the Bank Rate worked on the entire banking system, rather than on the clearing banks specifically. The role of the

London clearing banks as the conduit of monetary policy thus became less central.

In terms of the relationship between the state and the Bank of England, the Bank remained the central implementation of monetary policy after the introduction of CCC. It was the Bank which called for Special Deposits and Supplementary Special Deposits and monitored adherence to the reserve asset ratio across the whole banking system. Furthermore, given that a more monetarist approach implied a willingness to vary the Bank Rate as an instrument of monetary policy more pro-actively than in the recent past, in theory the Bank's influence would be enhanced. On 13 October 1972, however, just over a year after the introduction of CCC, the Bank Rate was replaced by the Minimum Lending Rate (MLR). The new rate was set not by the Court of Directors of the Bank of England in consultation with the Chancellor (as had been the Bank Rate) but was normally to be set at 0.5% above the average rate of discount for Treasury Bills established at the weekly tender. It was, therefore, more determined by the market than the Bank Rate and was thus in keeping with the philosophy of CCC. This denuded the Bank's role. Burnham interprets this change as an early experiment in the "rule-based depoliticisation" of monetary policy.[11] There was, however, a partial reversal of the experiment in March 1977 when it was determined that the Bank could override the MLR if it meant an "undesirable" reduction in the MLR.[12] In May 1978 the rate became a "fully administered rate" once again.

The context sketched out above gives an insight into pressures being brought to bear upon the postwar regulatory framework. Beginning around 1968 (with the merger of Westminster Bank with the National Provincial Bank and the ending of the "gentleman's agreement") and intensifying with CCC in September 1971, the dismantlement of the regulatory framework was underway.

This book concludes with two points of reflection for banks, bank regulators and regulatory policymakers in the light of this review of bank regulation from 1946 until 1971. First, as has been noted, banking crises have become more prevalent since the 1970s, certainly in comparison with the period between 1946 and the early 1970s. Laeven and Valencia put the number of banking crises globally in the period from 1970 to 2011 at 147.[13] To the extent that a stable banking system is one in which banking crises are absent, the period since the 1970s has been one of instability in banking, although measures taken since

2007–2009 in response to the global financial crisis may have been effective in slowing or reversing that trend. Stability is a guiding principle of the regulation of financial and banking systems because financial and banking crises can have severe social and economic consequences. The cost of the global financial crisis to the US economy over the period 2008–2023 has been "conservatively" estimated to be between $6 trillion and $14 trillion in 2012 dollars.[14] According to Eurostat, approved state aid measures in the EU between October 2008 and October 2010 in response to the crisis amounted to €4.6 trillion, while in 2009 alone the GDP of the EU contracted by 6% due to the crisis-induced recession.[15] In considering how best to manage the risk of banking crises, and manage the adverse consequences when they do occur, it is essential to reflect critically upon the efficacy of the approach to regulation adopted since the 1970s—one which relies heavily upon regulation in a highly codified form, and upon detailed and often highly technical rules.

Second, bank regulation is now being forged—certainly in the UK and possibly in many other countries—against the backdrop of a quite dramatic change in attitude towards banks since the 1980s. The *British Social Attitudes Survey* reported in 2013 on "perceptions of how well major institutions are run." In 1983, 90% of respondents regarded the banks as being well run. By 1994, the figure had fallen to 63% and by 2012 stood at just 19%. This was "probably the most dramatic change of attitude registered in 30 years of British Social Attitudes."[16] Insofar as being "well run" is an indicator that a bank is trustworthy, a plausible interpretation of this survey is that there has been a precipitous decline in the perceived trustworthiness of banks over the last three to four decades. Beyond the UK, an online global survey by the communications firm Edelman in late 2017 asked people how much they trusted businesses in fifteen different industry sectors "to do what is right." Only 54% of respondents trusted businesses in financial services "to do what is right," the lowest score of the fifteen sectors.[17] How can this perception—that banks are not trustworthy—be reversed? How can banks be encouraged or incentivized to strengthen their integrity, to improve their competence and to prove that their intentions are benevolent?[18] It is hoped that this review of a period of stability in banking contributes to bringing a historical perspective to bear on the these two pressing issues.

Notes

1. Glyn Davies, *A History of Money*, 3rd ed. (Cardiff: University of Wales Press, 2002; reprint, 2010): 414.
2. Committee on the Working of the Monetary System, *Report*, Cmnd. 827, August 1959, para. 198, Table 12.
3. Davies, *A History of Money*, 415.
4. Mae Baker and Michael Collins, "London as an International Banking Center, 1950–1980," in *London and Paris as International Financial Centres in the Twentieth Century*, ed. Youssef Cassis and Eric Bussière, Oxford Scholarship Online (Oxford: Oxford University Press, 2007): Table 12.1.
5. Ibid., Table 12.4.
6. *Bank of England Statistical Abstract 1992, Part 1: Banking, Capital Markets, Government Debt and Related Statistics, Interest and Exchange Rates* (London: Bank of England, 1992): Table 2: Banks in the United Kingdom: Balance Sheet of Monthly Reporting Institutions.
7. This prioritization is reflected in the Conservative Party's 1970 manifesto in *A Better Tomorrow: The Conservative Programme for the Next 5 Years*, 6, CPA PUB 156/1.
8. McCallum describes the different roles played by instruments, goals, intermediate targets and indicators in monetary policy. The instruments of monetary policy are those tools which are under the direct control of the authorities. In contrast, it is not possible to control intermediate targets, indicators or goals directly, at least to the same degree. See: Bennett T. McCallum, "Targets, Indicators, and Instruments of Monetary Policy, Working Paper No. 3047," *National Bureau of Economic Research* (July 1989): 3–5.
9. Duncan Needham, *UK Monetary Policy from Devaluation to Thatcher, 1967–82* (Basingstoke: Palgrave Macmillan, 2014): 21–45.
10. "The Importance of Money," *Bank of England Quarterly Bulletin* (Quarter 2, 1970): 159–98, accessed 24 August 2018, https://www.bankofengland.co.uk/-/media/boe/files/quarterly-bulletin/1970/the-importance-of-money.pdf. The paper is attributed to C. A. E. Goodhart with the assistance of A. D. Crockett.
11. Peter Burnham, "Depoliticising Monetary Policy: The Minimum Lending Rate Experiment in Britain in the 1970s," *New Political Economy* 16, no. 4 (2011): 464.
12. "Financial Review," *Bank of England Quarterly Bulletin* (Quarter 2, 1977): 163, accessed 24 August 2018, https://www.bankofengland.co.uk/-/media/boe/files/quarterly-bulletin/1977/financial-review-qb-1977-q2.pdf?la=en&hash=81EA8B07085AD7391453333B25C7F8627B099EC7.

13. Luc Laeven and Fabián Valencia, "Systemic Banking Crises Database: An Update, WP/12/163," in *IMF Working Papers* (International Monetary Fund, June 2012): 3.
14. Tyler Atkinson, David Luttrell, and Harvey Rosenblum, "How Bad Was It? The Costs and Consequences of the 2007–2009 Financial Crisis, Staff Papers No. 20," in Staff Papers (Federal Reserve Bank of Dallas, July 2013): 2.
15. "Capital Requirements—CRD IV/CRR—Frequently Asked Questions," *European Commission*, accessed 28 July 2018, http://europa.eu/rapid/press-release_MEMO-13-690_en.htm.
16. "British Social Attitudes 30, 2013 Edition," in *British Social Attitudes*, ed. A. Park et al. (London: NatCen Social Research, 2013): xvi, xv, accessed 20 August 2018, http://www.bsa.natcen.ac.uk/media/38723/bsa30_full_report_final.pdf.
17. *2018 Edelman Trust Barometer Global Report*, accessed 21 August 2018, http://cms.edelman.com/sites/default/files/2018-02/2018_Edelman_Trust_Barometer_Global_Report_FEB.pdf: 45. The 2018 Trust Barometer is their 18th annual trust and credibility survey. It measures trust across a number of institutions, sectors and geographies, surveying over 33,000 respondents across 28 countries.
18. Roger C. Mayer, James H. Davis, and F. David Schoorman, "An Integrative Model of Organizational Trust," *The Academy of Management Review* 20, no. 3 (July 1995): 717–20. Mayer, Davis and Schoorman suggest that ability, benevolence and integrity are the characteristics of a trustee which explain a major proportion of trustworthiness.

References

Secondary Sources

Books and Articles

British Social Attitudes 30, 2013 Edition British Social Attitudes, edited by A. Park, C. Bryson, E. Clery, J. Curtice, and M. Phillips. London: NatCen Social Research, 2013. Accessed 20 August 2018. http://www.bsa.natcen.ac.uk/media/38723/bsa30_full_report_final.pdf.

Atkinson, Tyler, David Luttrell, and Harvey Rosenblum. "How Bad Was It? The Costs and Consequences of the 2007–09 Financial Crisis, Staff Papers No. 20." *Staff Papers*, Federal Reserve Bank of Dallas, July 2013.

Baker, Mae, and Michael Collins. "London as an International Banking Center, 1950–1980." In *London and Paris as International Financial Centres in the Twentieth Century*, edited by Youssef Cassis and Eric Bussière, 1–23. Oxford: Oxford University Press, 2007. Accessed 15 February 2014. http://www.oxfordscholarship.com/view/10.1093/acprof:oso/9780199269495.001.0001/acprof-9780199269495-chapter-12.

Burnham, Peter. "Depoliticising Monetary Policy: The Minimum Lending Rate Experiment in Britain in the 1970s." *New Political Economy* 16, no. 4 (2011): 463–80.

Davies, Glyn. *A History of Money*. 3rd ed. Cardiff: University of Wales Press, 2002. Reprint, 2010.

Laeven, Luc, and Fabián Valencia. "Systemic Banking Crises Database: An Update, WP/12/163." *IMF Working Papers*, International Monetary Fund, June 2012. 1–32.

Mayer, Roger C., James H. Davis and F. David Schoorman. "An Integrative Model of Organizational Trust." *The Academy of Management Review* 20, no. 3 (July 1995): 709–34.

McCallum, Bennett T. "Targets, Indicators, and Instruments of Monetary Policy, Working Paper No. 3047." *National Bureau of Economic Research*, (July 1989): 1–42.

Needham, Duncan. *UK Monetary Policy from Devaluation to Thatcher, 1967–82*. Basingstoke: Palgrave Macmillan, 2014.

Index

© The Editor(s) (if applicable) and The Author(s), under exclusive licence to Springer Nature Switzerland AG 2018
L. Arch, *The Regulation of the London Clearing Banks, 1946–1971*, Palgrave Studies in Economic History,
https://doi.org/10.1007/978-3-030-00910-6

University of Reading Library

CPI Antony Rowe
Eastbourne, UK
December 20, 2018